Lessons, Laughter, and Tough Love: The Inez Clemmer Legacy

Written and Compiled by
Lettie Kirkpatrick Burress

Foreword by Dr. Paul Conn

Introduction by Alan Smith

Cover Art: Mural by Hollye Kile
Portrait by Aloha Buffington

Disclosure:
Every effort has been made to accurately portray the stories and
personalities referenced in these pages. Any errors are purely
unintentional and deeply regretted.

ISBN: 978-1-59684-260-1

Printed by *Derek Press*
Cleveland, Tennessee 37311

Without character all doors are closed, no matter how talented an individual may be or how much knowledge he may have. Character is not gained by taking certain courses, by reading good books, or by walking and talking with good friends. Character is the sum total of a person's reaction in meeting life's problems and emergencies.

Remember, your best chance for success in life rests in the quality of character you are developing. Make the decision now that character shall be your most important goal, and it shall be your greatest possession.

Ineg Clummer

The Ocoeean 1962

Contents

Foreword

Inez Clemmer was one of those rare individuals who, by the sheer force of her extraordinary personality, helped to shape the character of an entire community.

To describe Mrs. Clemmer merely as a teacher and high school administrator so understates the role she played in the lives of a generation of Bradley County young people that it hardly sounds familiar to those of us whose lives she touched. To us, she was a force of nature, and it is not an exaggeration to say that hundreds of us are whoever we are, to some degree, because our paths crossed hers at Bradley Central High School long ago.

Mrs. Clemmer served at Bradley Central during a time when it was the major high school in the county. (The other, in the days of racially segregated education, was College Hill School, attended by African-American students.) Students from both the Cleveland and Bradley County school systems were funneled into the same high school from all the city and county elementary schools, and the result was that whatever happened at BCHS had immediate and direct impact on the entire community.

At Bradley Central, all the various paths of nearly two thousand students -- rural kids who came in on yellow buses and joined the Future Farmers of America, city kids who walked to school from the nearby Ocoee Street neighborhoods, athletes on Bradley's championship teams, scholarly types from county and city who were focused on getting into selective colleges – all these paths shared one thing in common: their point of daily intersection was Mrs. Inez Clemmer. She was the center of gravity for the universe that we all occupied, and in one way or another, all our orbits spun around her.

There were other powerful personalities in the world of BCHS, to be sure. Coaches were important in a school so proud of its athletic teams. Many individual teachers cast giant shadows. To this day, forty years later, graduates of the classes of the 1960's still trace their intellectual lineage back to teachers like Lillie Frank Fitzgerald and Ross Apperson, who occupied separate ends of the Bradley building and exerted contrasting but powerful influences on their adoring students.

There were, of course, the high school principals with whom Mrs. Clemmer worked, all good men who served well, but who can hardly be blamed if they failed to leave their fingerprints on the lives of their students in the profound way of their assistant principal. While they were important as the CEO's of Bradley High, it was she who, in something of the role of a chief operating officer, mattered most in the day-to-day life of students at a personal level.

Mrs. Clemmer was a presence, literally and figuratively. Her office occupied the space at the school's main entrance and at the beginning and end of the day, and between classes, she could be seen standing there as students churned around her, seemingly missing nothing, seeing and hearing everything. During classes, she often walked the halls. We could sometimes hear her, as we sat quietly in civics or history or homeroom, the sound of her footsteps both a cautionary warning to behave and a reassuring reminder that the friendly neighborhood cop was on the beat.

She fully inhabited the place.

Mrs. Clemmer was not "just" an administrator. She was also a teacher, a very good one who expected and got strong performance from her students. She taught Latin, and felt that every college-bound student should take it. I arrived at BCHS in the tenth grade, along with my classmates from the city system, having spent ninth grade at Arnold Junior High School. There we had a less-than-stellar experience in Latin I. Our class as a whole generally frittered away the year. In the summer before entering Bradley High, we became alarmed, as a group, that we were unprepared for the legendary toughness of Inez Clemmer, awaiting us in Latin II. We actually had group cramming sessions at Arnold that summer, trying to make up for lost time.

When the school year arrived, I choked. Among my underachieving Latin I classmates, I was the chief underachiever, and I had heard tales of how difficult Latin II could be under Mrs. Clemmer. So on the first day of classes that fall, I dropped Latin II and signed up for first-year Spanish instead. A few days after classes began, as I was walking down the hallway at the end of the day, I passed Mrs. Clemmer's office. She was standing outside in the corridor, as she so often did.

She greeted me by name. (I was surprised she knew who I was, although I had an older brother and sister who preceded me at Bradley, and whom she knew well. They had told me many Mrs.

Clemmer stories.) She apparently recognized me from the family resemblance. "You're Paul Conn, aren't you?" she said.

"Yes, ma'am."

"Well, young man, we are glad to have you at Bradley," she said. And then, with no warning, she revealed she knew more than just my name. "I'm disappointed you've dropped Latin," she said. "What was your reason for doing that?"

Uh oh. "Well," I hesitated, trying to think, "I signed up for Spanish instead."

"And why would you do that?" she persisted.

"Well, I've always wanted to speak Spanish, and I couldn't take both."

Mrs. Clemmer went straight for the kill. "I certainly hope it's not because you think Latin is too hard," she said. "You didn't do very well in first-year Latin, did you?" Then without waiting for an answer, she said, "I hope you didn't dodge my class just because you're looking for the easy way out."

Busted. She saw through me perfectly. That was Mrs. Clemmer. I doubt it was true that she could actually read a student's mind, but it sure seemed that way sometimes.

That first encounter with Inez Clemmer typified what I and many other students saw in her on a consistent basis for all those many years. She was incredibly observant and insightful; she knew and remembered students on a personal basis; she took an interest in them and held them to a high standard; and she always told the truth in an unflinching way that made us want to please her and meet her expectations. She was more than just a teacher of Latin; she was a teacher of life. She went way beyond being an administrator; she was a person who framed the daily decisions of our lives in a way that connected even our ordinary behaviors to the issues of our personal character.

I was so pleased when I learned that this book was being prepared, a book that tells "Mrs. Clemmer stories", but does so in the context of the basic principles that were so important to her. It is a perfect approach. It will introduce this phenomenal lady to a new generation of Cleveland and Bradley County students, in a manner that emphasizes the concepts and values which she both taught and exemplified.

In reading the early draft of this book, I learned things about her as a person, things about her own background, which I never knew before. As high school students, we strangely never thought much about her personal life. I don't even remember wondering -- I would no more have wondered about Inez Clemmer's personal affairs than about the personal life of the Statue of Liberty. She was so much larger than life; she seemed beyond those small details, and I think her students couldn't grasp the concept that she with a history and a life apart from the domain of Bradley High, was once a young girl.

For those who knew her, this book will bring warm reminders of what we remember, as well as tell us things we never knew. For those who missed the pleasure of being one of her students, it will be a wonderful introduction.

She was one of a kind, Inez Clemmer. Who can calculate the impact she made, through all those students, which radiates even today throughout the community of Cleveland and Bradley County? The ripples on the pond will continue forever.

Dr. Paul Conn, President
Lee University

Preface

I'm glad to have had the privilege of compiling, editing, and polishing this book detailing the life, legacy, and contributions of Inez Clemmer. This work has also seemed somehow appropriate, since I was in the graduating class that saw Mrs. Clemmer's retirement. The rowdy students in the class of 1969 sometimes referred to themselves as the class that ran off Inez Clemmer! Some bragged that we "did her in". We all knew better, of course.

I also am pleased to participate in this project because Mrs. Clemmer contributed to open doors for me, as she did for so many others. My family was fragmented and I had little hope of college. But, one day, a Cleveland State financial aid counselor visited Bradley High and asked to see *me*! As for so many others, the unexpected doors opened and I walked through, courtesy of several BCHS adults who believed in my potential.

Perhaps the true gift of this book for me has been the realization of several insights.

- A life well lived has incredible ripple effects through time and generations.
- Even a person's later years can be filled with great contribution, delightful relationships, and multiple opportunities to continue impacting lives.
- "Community" is a powerful concept and to "belong" is a privilege.

A diligent team has been committed to excellence in working on this project. It seemed daunting at times. But, we are excited about the results and truly expect *Lessons, Laughter, and Tough Love: The Inez Clemmer Legacy* to be both a keepsake and a community treasure. To be able to offer it to our students as proof that real character not only makes a difference, but leaves a legacy, has made it worth all the effort.

Lettie Kirkpatrick Burress

Acknowledgements

Special recognition is owed to those who expressed appreciation to Inez Clemmer through writings placed in an "Appreciation Book" in March of 1985 and to those who made the effort to present their memories to the committee for use in this tribute. Many stories came from Bradley County and others from across the United States. Some stories came with laughter, while others came with tears. All came with a deep regard for a remarkable lady.

The family of Inez Clemmer, Don Smith, Gary Smith, Marguerite Smith, Kent Smith, Alan Smith, Leslie Smith Christian, and Lindsey Smith were very supportive. Their cooperation in supplying family pictures and personal moments was invaluable.

Thanks go to Melinda Martin and Kathy Murray Morelock of the Bill Schultz Library at Bradley Central High School for assistance in photo editing/scanning and Ocoeean searches. Maureen Olsson Lovelace and Wanda Shults from Ocoee Middle School provided their skill in editing and proofing. Lebron Montgomery from the Bradley County Schools Central Office assisted with the character education aspect of the project. Nancy Eskew, Peggy Meyer, and Amy Slifko, library volunteers, and Joyce Ratcliff, library assistant, provided a variety of helpful services.

Finally, many thanks to Lettie Jones Kirkpatrick Burress who pulled together the pieces to organize, write, and compile a menagerie into an enjoyable, readable, and heartfelt tribute.

We acknowledge, with regret, that there are many more stories that should have been told.

Inez Clemmer Library Committee

Introduction

My earliest memories of Inez were in the days that followed her retirement from teaching; I was eight or so. Living just a few blocks away, a daily summer ritual for my brother, sisters and me was to go to "Aunt Inez's" for a cola and visit. On the weekends, we took turns spending the night at her house. The evening normally consisted of a dinner of our choice and watching television. We capped things off with a game of checkers and a bible story.

Inez and her husband Lee loved to walk our neighborhood, and we were always on the lookout for them. It wasn't that we did great and exciting things that made us want to be with Inez; it was the way Inez made us feel when we were with her. She made us feel special, that no one else mattered and that we could and would do great things. I suspect her students felt the same. Over time, our summer afternoons and sleepovers were replaced with evening visits with my wife and family and, finally, working lunches. I had lunch with Inez the Friday before her life-ending stroke on Sunday. She was ninety-five.

While Inez led a fulfilled life, she did not escape life's trials and tribulations, Like all of us, she experienced hard times and heartaches. She lost her only child at birth. When her sister Frances died at an early age, Inez became the mother figure to Frances's two sons Don and Gary. Finally, the last years of Lee's life were very difficult as he lost his abilities to function and Inez, in the twilight of her own life, was once again a caregiver.

Even as her own health began to fail, her focus on others and her values never changed. I never heard Inez complain about anybody or anything. She was always positive and happy. I think she understood that life was not supposed to always be easy and fun and that while life's choices and circumstances might be difficult at times, they really aren't when viewed with solid values. Lastly, I think Inez benefited from the deepest of all satisfactions: that her time here was well spent and that her life had mattered, an appropriate reward for a life well lived.

What is character and does it really matter? Further, is reaching a high moral character an end in itself or does it serve some other purpose? As mankind has attempted to understand how to behave and live, these questions have occupied the thoughts and energies of history's best minds. I think my Aunt Inez discovered that the only way to approach the world and its challenges was with the protection and guidance of a strong set of values collectively called character.

In the pages that follow, you will find values and traits that define character. You will discover the life of a remarkable lady who lived by those traits and who was rewarded with a life of happiness, as well as the love and admiration of those that knew her.

Alan Smith,
Great-nephew of Inez Clemmer

CHAPTER 1

A WOMAN OF INFLUENCE

"There is no one in Bradley County who has touched as many lives."

- Jack Brown, former student

"There is no one in Bradley County who has touched as many lives."

That is what Jack Brown, a former student, believes about Inez Clemmer. He could be correct, as Mrs. Clemmer's legacy did not just span the students that she impacted in her 30 year career as educator and assistant principal at Bradley Central High School. Her influence lives on in their families and in this community. As the ideals and character that she both modeled and demanded are taught in our schools and homes, the powerful imprint of her life is undeniable.

Her Roots

Some of Mrs. Clemmer's students could not imagine that she even had a family, apparently believing her world was Bradley Central High School. One student, G.P. Tulloss, was surprised to discover a Clemmer family connection. He later indicated, "I must have thought you were manufactured and had no relatives". Perhaps some family history would dispel that myth.

Hettie Inez Higgins (Mrs. Clemmer) was born in Polk

 County, Tennessee, March 6, 1907. She was the third of seven children born to Frederick Dyke and Martha Catherine Dunn Higgins. Although her mother's family was from Murray Country, Georgia, her dad's people were original settlers in Polk County. Mrs. Clemmer's siblings were Lester (who died in infancy), Mary Lou Lillard, Wallace, Frances Smith, Roy, Ralph, and Kenneth. When Mrs. Clemmer was twenty, her mom died.

A 1926 graduate of Carson Newman College, Mrs. Clemmer returned home to Polk County where she taught at both Ducktown and Polk County High Schools. She also coached girls' basketball.

Lee and Inez Clemmer

In 1936 she married Lee Clemmer, also from Polk County. They later moved to Bradley County where she taught math and Latin and also served as assistant principal until her retirement in 1969. Inez and Lee Clemmer had only one child, a daughter, Nancy, who died in infancy.

Lady Clemmer

In marrying Lee Clemmer, who was employed at Magic Chef, Mrs. Clemmer found not only a spouse, but a bridge partner. These two were serious players. Mrs. Clemmer also had a standing date with friends who remember her skills at duplicate bridge. She is described as being "sharp as a tack" and "a delightful lady who never got upset".

Perhaps Mrs. Clemmer's faith offers some explanation for the power and influence of her life. Mrs. Clemmer's niece, Leslie, remembers her aunt's faithfulness to her church, Broad Street Methodist. She also recalls her love for and knowledge of the Bible. As a child, she often turned to her Aunt Inez when she had questions about faith and the scriptures.

Teacher Clemmer

Inez Clemmer, The Ocoeean 1958

Although Mrs. Clemmer's reputation as an incredible assistant principal is legendary, many lives were also impacted by her great skills as a Latin and math teacher. Sylvia Lauderdale Coates remembers her great delight in discovering that the stern, demanding, assistant principal became a "sensitive, brilliant, loving teacher" in Latin class. She gives a glowing account of this teacher who "motivated, educated, and intrigued us all". They were "spellbound to her vivid mythology" as she "brought a dead language to life and simultaneously inspired us to use our minds, to be productive, and to pursue excellence".

Another student, Joy Bush Orr, recalls that just walking into her classroom gave me an awesome feeling of being in a learning atmosphere". Phyllis Wright was inspired by

Mrs. Clemmer to become a teacher herself. Now retired from BCHS, she still considers Inez Clemmer to be her role model for what a teacher should be.

One of Mrs. Clemmer's success stories is Tommy Lee from the class of 1955. Tommy Lee had Mrs. Clemmer for two years of Algebra and two years of Latin. He served in the Air Force as an intelligence agent in the Russian language. Tommy comments, "The Air Force trained me, but I was selected in part on the two years of Latin. I later became an engineer and the Algebra was the building blocks for other math. The most important thing I learned from being in Mrs. Clemmer's classes was the ability to think about the problems and understand what the thing I was looking for was".

Equally significant is how she loved what she did. Her nephew Gary Smith remembers, "She told me that despite a weekend for relaxation and preparation, she could hardly wait to return to Bradley High and to the classroom. Contrary to most of us who long for the weekend, she thrived on the 'weekdays' from which she derived her greatest joy, pleasure and satisfaction".

Mother Clemmer

Although the Clemmers did not raise children of their own, her maternal instincts found no shortage of outlets. Her own siblings needed her nurture and certainly Bradley High students were the recipients of her fierce protection and training — the yearbook tribute at her retirement speaks of "her motherly concern for her 'children' ".

The "tough and tender" side of Mrs. Clemmer will be addressed in a later chapter. However, no book about Mrs. Clemmer's legacy would be accurate without acknowledging her great influence even beyond the classroom and principal's office. Though this book will pay tribute to the amazing significance of that era of her life, her family found her presence in their lives to be equally powerful and very much welcome.

Mrs. Clemmer's mothering capacity was apparently limitless and it was definitely welcomed in the lives of her two nephews, Don and Gary Smith. The Clemmer move to Cleveland proved especially timely to them following the loss of their mother. Aunt Inez became their surrogate mother figure.

Inez Clemmer with great-great nieces and nephews 1998
L-R Kent Christian, Megan Smith, Inez, Miles Christian, Caroline Smith, Katie Smith,
Parker Smith

As her nephew Gary married and had children, she and Lee became like grandparents to those children. Here again, she proved herself a person of uncommon influence. Her great-nieces and nephews, Kent, Alan, Leslie, and Lindsey paid tribute to their "Aunt Inez" in a letter written after her death and read at her funeral.

They spoke of her contribution to their lives with her strong maternal presence, as well as acknowledging her community of admirers. As did all who knew her, they recognized the higher standard she set for them, which was also characteristic of her own life.

Perhaps a fitting and true closing of this intro chapter would be to share the summary from this family letter:

"Aunt Inez, most people spend a lifetime looking for someone to help them through the daily challenges, frustrations, and sometimes heartaches of life. To help them find meaning, hope, and direction in what at times can be a very confusing world. Some people find that help from a parent or spouse, but many people found that help from you. You were certainly more than teacher, you were a dear friend to everyone you knew.

Today we mourn your passing, but more importantly we celebrate your wonderful life. We are all truly better off having loved you and will face tomorrow a little wiser and braver knowing that a little of you is in each of us."

The Ocoeean 1959

CHAPTER 2

A WOMAN OF RESPECT

Respect: Showing high regard for authority, country, self, and others. Treating others as you would want to be treated. The understanding that all people have value as human beings.

Respect for ourselves guides our morals. Respect for others guides our manners.

- Laurence Sterne

A Vision of Greatness

She had a vision for every child and that was what I thought was uniquely special about Mrs. Clemmer.

- Herbert Lackey

For Inez Clemmer respect was always a two way street. It is clear that her very presence . . . or even the sound of her approaching presence . . . or even the threat of her possible presence, definitely commanded respect. Yet, the true power of respect in her life was not so much that she received it, but that she gave it even to those under her authority. More amazing, she gave it based on her "vision of greatness" for what she saw a student could become. She saw past the often struggling, insecure, circumstance- bound, immature, and sometimes rebellious adolescents at Bradley Central High School and fixed instead on who they could be.

As some of these stories will indicate that vision made all the difference. Other stories will just serve as examples of the give and take of respect for and from Mrs. Clemmer, reminding us all that respect really does matter.

Yep, every morning, she was there smiling with the paddle under her arm and saying, "Good morning, children".

- Joyce Self Shook

The Fruit of Respect

Herbert Lackey

I am going to tell you about a person who changed my life. It helps to understand where I came from, where I have tried to go. I came to Bradley High School in 1953. My dad told me that he never attended a day of school in his life. He was a self-educated man. He read three newspapers a day. He was self taught. My mom told me she went to the fifth grade.

We lived out in the country. We had no electricity, no refrigerator. We had a mule. We farmed. We grew stuff and sold it. We were poor economically, but rich in loving and caring and dreaming. We had a positive lifestyle.

I attended a tiny elementary school. Some years we had one in class, sometimes two. It contained all eight grades in one. The first library I had opportunity to walk into and check out books was BCHS.

I first met Mrs. Clemmer when I came to Bradley High and was in the office getting my admittance form. She looked at my name and said, "Lackey. I knew a Herbert L. Lackey. I went to school with him at Polk County High School in 1927, I believe."

That was my uncle. He had died before he finished high school. My granddad had owned a store in Polk County. Then the depression came and people took everything from him, but couldn't pay. He had gone into bankruptcy and had to move to Hamilton County. Mrs. Clemmer knew some of these things. Now she said, "I am really glad to meet you," and told me several good things about my family.

From that day on I would see Mrs. Clemmer and she would call me by my name. For a poor kid to be called by name, you just can't believe what that felt like to me. I just couldn't wait to see Mrs. Clemmer because she recognized me. The power of a teacher is just incredible.

She said things like, "You ought to run for student council president." So I did. I actually won. She saw things in me that I had no way of recognizing for myself. She believed in me and I sensed that. As time went on she said, "Where are you going to go to college?"

Now I am almost embarrassed to say that I had not even heard of the University of Tennessee. She said, "You need to go to college" and she talked to me about where I could go and where I could get help. She had me believing I could do it. So I did go to college. I did graduate. And I came back to BCHS as a teacher.

As a student, I knew of the high expectations she held for ALL students. I observed the tremendous respect in which other Bradley faculty and staff members held her.

- Jerry Frazier

No Nicknames

G.P. Tulloss

All students, I guess, have had nicknames for many of their teachers . . . names such as "Speedy", "Bozo", "Shorty", and "Foxy". It wasn't out of disrespect, it was just one of those high school things. However, I felt a certain amount of fear in the presence of Mrs. Clemmer. She was always Mrs. Clemmer . . . not even Miss Clemmer. Many married teachers came to accept "Miss" rather than "Mrs." because it seemed fruitless to attempt to correct our pronunciation of "Mrs." There was no such thing as a "Ms." between 1945 and 1949, so we didn't have that option. She was "Mis'iz" Clemmer.

Mrs. Clemmer taught me more than the correct pronunciation of "Mrs.". It came as a surprise when I found out, as a senior in high school, that an "arsh" potato was, in fact, an Irish potato!

A great role model for the firm, but fair, teacher Mrs. Clemmer also challenged and encouraged. She made us secretly proud that she could control our class. Very few teachers could control the class of '49.

> *As a beginning teacher in 1966-67 at BCHS, I tried to be correct in my pronunciation. One day Mrs. Clemmer heard me use Mrs. and pronounce it incorrectly. She quietly, but authoritatively, said, "Mr. Reno, that is pronounced Misses, not Miseries."*
> *- Harold Reno*

Bill McClure

Mrs. Clemmer was probably the most respected educator I've ever been around. At our 30th class reunion, I was the Master of Ceremonies and we were talking and laughing about the nicknames we had for all our teachers. There were several funny ones about teachers and even the principal, but I commented to the class that I knew Mrs. Clemmer's nickname was Mrs. Clemmer because we wouldn't dare call her anything else!

Mrs. Clemmer was not just a name, she was a presence, she was a force. She was the personality that loomed over this place.
- Paul Conn

Guilt by Association

Eddie Cartwright

Inez Clemmer was one of the people that had an influence on my life. I was never actually in her classroom, but she was a sister to Coach Smith's wife and I played basketball for Coach Smith and she always showed an interest in us boys. She wanted to make sure that we made the grades we were supposed to make.

I can remember even after graduation some of us hung out at the local pool hall. I was there one day --- now a freshman in college --- on a day off. About three or four of the guys from Bradley came in. Well, it wasn't long until Mrs. Clemmer was on their trail and into the poolroom she came. They commenced to hide and whatever, and you know, out of respect, I almost was ready to go hide myself!

She loaded those boys up and took them back to school. I am sure they felt her wrath in that detention hall because she was good at taking care of the business at Bradley High School.

Somehow as we grow older, and hopefully more mature, we cherish even more the realization that without the guidance and help of certain people in our lives, our lives may have very well taken a negative course.

- Bill Arnold, M.D.

Respecting the Rules

Josephine Day

I was somewhat of a rebel and got kicked out of several classes for my stubborn behavior. However, this story is not about my rebellion, but about a misunderstanding.

In 1940 a rule was made that anyone getting married after the Christmas holidays would have to quit school. I couldn't make Conrad

> *I can still picture, thirty years later, her standing in the hall of Bradley, as classes changed. Her very presence brought civility to the halls. When I think of respect for a teacher, I think of Mrs. Clemmer. She was dignity personified.*
> *- Linda Mital McConnell*

believe that and he insisted we marry on January 25, 1941. We kept it a good secret until I graduated.

Conrad was circulation manager for the Chattanooga Times in Athens. On Monday mornings after the business meeting in Chattanooga, he would drive by Bradley at lunch time on his way to Athens. I would go sit in the car with him during the lunch period.

One Monday the rule was made that sitting in cars with boys at lunch time would not be allowed. However, Conrad was supposed to come by at lunch and there was no way to notify him. So at lunch, I went out as usual to sit in the car and tell him of the rule. Mrs. Clemmer walked by the car and saw us. I appreciated the fact that she did not embarrass me in front of him.

However when the bell rang, as expected, I was called to the office. Mrs. Clemmer warned me of the rule. I never said a word because I couldn't tell her that I was not sitting with my boyfriend, but with my husband!

There may have been times that we resented your iron-clad rules of discipline, but we all knew that those rules taught us respect for authority, justice, and humanity.

- *Markolita Still Vaden*

Telling It Like It Is

Paul Conn

The last good conversation I had with Mrs. Clemmer as a student was close to graduation. I was the editor of our school paper, *The Trumpeter*. The newspaper office was at the end of the hall and we got off one school period to work on the paper. We could also hang out and goof off there.

I was down there by myself late in my senior year when it got deathly quiet in the hall. The old building had wood floors and Mrs. Clemmer kind of walked in a stiff way. She always wore these good heavy duty shoes. She did not glide quietly down the hall. She came down with authority.

Standing in the room, I could hear those steps. She came down into the room where I was and said she wanted to talk to me for a few moments. She closed the door behind her. I saw in her a warmth and love that I have carried with me since.

She said, "You are getting ready to leave here and you have had a good time at Bradley. However, there are two or three things I want to remind you about. First of all, Paul, you wait to the last minute to do everything and one of these days it is going to get you. Don't wait till the last minute just because you can do it fast." One other thing she said was, "The thing I admire about you is you don't mind being who you are. I want to encourage you to keep being who you are, work hard, and good things will happen."

Most Likely to Succeed
Paul Conn
The Ocoeean 1963

Inez Clemmer Library
Presentation to students
October, 2003

You expected us to do our best and you taught us that this was possible both through our own character and your respect and confidence in us.

- Jeanette Manly Schlaeger

CHAPTER 3

A WOMAN OF RESPONSIBILITY

Responsibility: Being accountable in word and deed. Having a sense of duty to fulfill tasks with reliability, dependability and commitment.

The price of greatness is responsibility.
                                        - Winston Churchill

The pool hall boys?

The Ocoeean 1952

Where the "In Crowd" stays...

The Ocoeean 1953

Chasing the Prodigals

Don't ever do anything that you are ashamed to put your name on.
- Inez Clemmer to Paul Conn

Perhaps, if Mrs. Clemmer had one primary passion for the training of her students at BCHS, it would have been to see them grow in the area of responsibility. She would, without compromise, hold them accountable for the choices they made. She made certain they knew to expect to "pay the piper" for the wrong choices. Equally so, she enthusiastically affirmed their good decisions.

As these stories, both humorous and poignant, will demonstrate, Mrs. Clemmer did not shirk her own commitment to the duties of assistant principal and teacher. She faithfully modeled responsibility and all its components. For Mrs. Clemmer this often did mean "chasing the prodigals" from pool halls, parking lots, restrooms — and even gas stations. Those students who experienced her "mentoring" in this area also carried into their communities and lives the "marks" (and memories) of her determined tutoring in the area of personal accountability and responsibility.

No Place to Hide

Jeanne Harshbarger Sawyer

My friends and I decided to cut a class and go to the Bradley Snack Shop across the street. That is where we hung out before, during, and after school. It had booths with very high backs and there were other tables on the other side. We were in the booths and just having a ball, when someone said, "Here comes Mrs. Clemmer".

We all jumped up and ran toward the back booth, getting down under the table on the floor. Mrs. Clemmer came through the front door and asked the manager if anyone was there. Well, it wasn't long before Mrs. Clemmer was down on the floor getting us out from under the table. She then walked us all back across the street to class.

Berta McReynolds Silcox

I remember an incident told to me by other classmates. It seems Mack's Pool Hall was downtown Cleveland and a very popular hangout for high school boys. Mrs. Clemmer had an uncanny ability to identify the students who would skip class to spend time at the pool hall. She would then fling open the pool hall door and yell at the students to return to class.

They would run into the bathroom and stand on the toilet seats to hide from her. That, however, did not stop her. She never failed in her endeavor to return all those students to the classroom

Many of these boys have become prominent businessmen in the community. Who knows what kind of influence she had on their lives?

Brenda Beaty Remine

You can't reflect on high school without Mrs. Clemmer, and for those of us who knew her "personally", you can't help but smile. My story has to do with my self-appointed three lunch periods. I had Physical Education during the first two lunch periods, so I skipped class most days with the excuse that I had "cramps". I would go over to the snack shop and dance till my real lunch period which was the third period.

One day while I was dancing with Bill Edwards, Buddy Brock, and Webb Smalling, I spotted Mrs. Clemmer coming across the street. I decided to duck my head out the side door --- I somehow knew she was coming for me. As I watched her get close to the door, I made my getaway . . . and ran smack into her!

She had this twinkle in her eye and a sly smile and said, "I was just on the phone with your mother and she and I think that you might need a check-up since you are having so much trouble with your monthly cycles!" I never could figure out how one minute she was coming through the front door and then WHAM! – in two seconds, she was at the side door.

John Climer

The year was 1960, my sophomore year at Bradley. There was a service station at the corner of APD 40 and Ocoee Street where Walgreens is now. It was called Rodrick's Service Station. I went to school with Donald Rodrick, the boy whose dad owned that station.

One day Don and I decided to skip school and help out around the station. About 12:30 in the afternoon, this real shiny 1959 Chevy pulled in. Donnie and I ran out the door to do our jobs. I went to wash the windshield as Donnie inquired, "How much ma'am?"

All of a sudden, Don said, "John, we've got trouble." I walked over to discover that the car we had insisted on taking from Mr. Rodrick was the car of the one and only Inez Clemmer. She said nothing except, "Fill'er up boys, and I'll see you in my office first thing tomorrow morning!"

Well, at 9:00 A.M. sharp, over the intercom came Mrs. Clemmer's voice. "Johnny Climer and Donald Roderick report to the office immediately." When we got there, Mrs. Clemmer said, "Boys, I've decided that since y'all like workin' at the station better than comin' to school, I'm gonna let ya'll work there for the rest of the week."

After we realized we were suspended, we left and headed for the station. But before we could get out the door, Mrs. Clemmer hollered, "I don't want ya'll back here till Monday either!"

Bobby Houlk

In the early 1950's, Bradley had a daytime ballgame (during school hours) in Chattanooga. Half of the school signed up to go to the ballgame. Mrs. Clemmer knew that many kids did not have transportation to the game.

So she walked down to Bob's Pool Hall on Church Street, across from the Bradley County Agricultural Office, and found a lot of her students there. When she walked in, the boys ran for the bathroom. This did not stop Mrs. Clemmer. She went in after them. She marched me and the rest of the kids up Ocoee Street and back to school.

When she called to check on students it was just a confirmation call. She always knew where they were. She knew more about some of them than their own parents did.

- Blair Cunnyngham

The TWO That Got Away

Ronald Rogers

We (Ralph Pippenger and I) were cutting class at the Snack Shop. We saw Mrs. Clemmer coming from the school. We waited until she came in the front door. We went out the side door at the same time.

In the process of running through Clifton Duff's back yard, Pip ran into a clothesline (metal), knocking him off his feet. He got up and we made THE GREAT ESCAPE.

No Smoking Zone

Joy Self Shook

To me, Mrs. Clemmer was a big woman. She seemed tall. She used to walk the halls, searching for kids out of their classrooms and for girls smoking in the restrooms

She always seemed to have plenty of detention to pass out and she did so freely. If she thought we were carrying cigarettes in our purses, she'd call you into her office and search your purse. If any were found, she'd take them out, throw them in the trash and give you a lecture on how "it's not lady-like to be smoking".

Marguerite Miles Smith

I remember only too well sitting on the gym back steps where I thought no one ever frequented. As I sat there smoking a cigarette, I heard this firm voice say, "Miss Miles, where are you supposed to be now?" Well, what I wanted was for the earth to open and swallow me whole.

Exposed

Norma Davis Coppinger

I had been at Bradley nearly four years and had not skipped school until the latter part of my senior year. At that time, three of my best friends, Joan Whettemore Barrett, Shirley Ruth, Linda May, and I decided we needed to experience this at least once before we graduated.

Joan was married and we spent the night with her. We read books, told jokes, and laughed until time for school to be out. We walked home just like always. When I went into the house, my mother was waiting for me. She gave me the third degree about my day at school. I told her I had been in school.

She reached over and got the Bible and proceeded to read me some scriptures about lying . . . I didn't realize why she chose the scripture. After she finished reading the Bible to me, she said, "I know that you were not in school today, Mrs. Clemmer called to ask if you were sick". Well, no sleep that night for worrying about facing Mrs. Clemmer.

The next morning the four of us reported to the office at eight o'clock sharp. We were so afraid we felt sick to our stomachs . . . we did expect the worst. We assured Mrs. Clemmer, this being our senior year, it would never happen again. Since we had never been in trouble before, we received a week's detention. But it was a very long week.

I now realize that the certainty that Mrs. Clemmer would find out suppressed much unacceptable behavior.
- Markolita Still Vaden

A Name is a Name

Johnny Gregg

I was always being called up to the office. There was another boy named "Johnny Gregg". He was always getting into trouble, but they would send for me instead of him. As soon as she saw me, she would send me back to class and go get the other boy. It was pretty funny because I would be called out of homeroom almost every other morning to go to Mrs. Clemmer's office.

The most threatening thing to us students in the late 1950's and early 1960's was not nuclear war, drugs, or child abuse. The worse thing we could imagine was being sent to the office of Mrs. Inez Clemmer.
- Sylvia Lauderdale Coates

I Know Who You Are

Paul Conn

I remember a time when Mrs. Clemmer chewed me out royally for something I had done. Three or four students had broken into the cafeteria and vandalized it. Afterwards there were some angry responses about these high school kids, how they were delinquents, disrespectful, and out of control.

So I wrote a letter to the Banner and chewed out all the grown-ups for thinking that all the young people were bad. I wrote that the kids at Bradley were great and we were tired of being blamed for everything. I signed the letter, "a Bradley student". I didn't tell anyone that I wrote it.

But the next day after the letter appeared, Mrs. Clemmer sent a note, asking me to come see her. When I went in her office and closed the door, she said, "Young man, I want to talk to you about this letter you wrote to the Cleveland Daily Banner." I couldn't lie to Mrs. Clemmer. I said, "How did you know I wrote it?"

She said, "Did you think I would read this letter and not know who wrote it? There was only one person at Bradley High School who could have written this letter and that is you."

> *You helped me take the right paths when I would have taken the wrong one. I will always remember you as the lady who corrected my errors.*
>
> *- Janey Parton*

She continued, "Don't ever write a letter where you accuse somebody of doing something that you are doing yourself. You are accusing all the grown-ups of being down on all the teenagers and, in fact, you are characterizing all the grown-ups. And besides that, don't ever do anything that you are ashamed to put your name on."

It was like the voice of God. She read it and figured it out and nailed me.

Her powers of intuition are legendary.
- Nancy Carney, Cleveland Daily Banner

Tough on Teachers . . . Sometimes

Bill Schultz

I can't remember his name, so we'll call him Jimmy. He was one of the football coaches. He wasn't very tall --- he was pretty short and chunky. He was loved by the students and Mrs. Clemmer thought a lot of him, too.

At that time, like today, we had a lot of reports that were due daily. There was one report that had to be sent in at the close of the day. Jimmy failed to get the report in a time or two and she gave him a pretty good reprimand. For a few days he got the report in on time, and then he forgot again. However, school was out and he couldn't get it in.

In the old school, Mrs. Clemmer's office had one front door that was the only way out and right beside the door was a window, and it was pretty far off the floor. So Jimmy decided he was going to get that report in early. He planned to get to school before anyone and get that window open and get into her office with the report.

Well he climbed up, got the window open, and was halfway in and halfway out. Now it just so happened that Mrs. Clemmer came early and had gotten there first. When she walked in, there was Jimmy with his feet out in the hall, hung in the window, and his head in her office.

So she came in and just closed the window on him. But from then on, Jimmy always got that report in on time.

Harold Reno

As a first year teacher, I lost my book numbers for books checked out to students. I told Mrs. Clemmer what I had done and asked her what to do. She said, "Fake it. Most of the students will find their books."

So, I called each name and wrote down their book numbers. Sure enough, only two books were lost.

You could always count on her to stand behind a teacher, when that was needed.

- Maxine Gannaway Hyde

Excuses, Excuses, Confessions

Bill McClure

During my junior year of high school I had been out sick, but forgot to get a note from my mother. When I got to school the next morning I hurried to the agriculture department and asked a friend of mine to write me a note. He wrote:

> *Mrs. Clemmer,*
>   *Please excuse Bill from school yesterday. He was sick.*
>   *Mrs. McClure*

I took the note to Mrs. Clemmer, received my excused absence, and went on to class. However, during first period an announcement came over the intercom: "Bill McClure, please report to Mrs. Clemmer's office." With a great deal of apprehension, I followed instructions.

When I arrived at her office, Mrs. Clemmer said, "Bill, your mother called just a minute ago – she said she forgot to give you a note for your absence yesterday. Now do you want to tell me who wrote the note for you?"

I said, "Mrs. Clemmer, you know I can't tell you that."

To that she replied, "I guess I would have been disappointed if you had told me."

I did get to keep the excuse, but I also got two hours of detention to go with it.

Now, after twenty-seven years, I feel compelled to cleanse my conscience and let everyone know the identity of the "terrible person" who wrote that note for me. It was none other than the man who is nationally recognized as being the best agriculture teacher in the entire United States. It is the man who has helped guide the local Vo-Ag Department to consecutive National Gold Emblems since he has been part of the program.

Thank you, Herb.*

* (reference to Herbert Lackey)

Junior Sleuth

Deborah Humberd Kimsey

Being one of Mrs. Clemmer's office aides afforded me the opportunity to learn many things from her tutelage. Not only did she command respect, responsibility, and honesty from me, she expected it from others.

If office aides allowed a student to leave in error, we were responsible for finding the student. Back in the days before cell phones, this was not always an easy task. When I couldn't find a student, it was double-trouble for me as we were held *accountable*. I spent a lot of time tracking down students who I had let leave for a few minutes that never returned. Tom Johnson was usually easy to find as I could count on him to be on his way to Cleveland High to see Judi. Some of the students, though, were very good at conning me and were very, very elusive. . . I still haven't found Michael Penney.

My classmates and I discovered that Miss Inez took her responsibilities very seriously and expected us to do the same.
- Ruthanna Stratton Almond

Assistant Principal
MRS. INEZ CLEMMER

The Ocoeean 1958

CHAPTER 4

A WOMAN OF PERSEVERANCE

Perseverance: Pursuing worthy objectives with determination and patience while exhibiting fortitude when confronted with failure.

Perseverance is a great element of success. If you only knock long enough and loud enough at the gate you are sure to wake somebody.

- Henry Wadsworth Longfellow

The Mighty Motivator

*One thing she knew about me was that I was not a quitter and that
I would not give up.*

- Stony Brooks

The character of her students mattered to Inez Clemmer.
It mattered a lot. Her hopes for their future drove her to demand
their best, to hold them accountable, and to refuse to let them give
in to their circumstances. As she saw their potential, she steered
them toward success. When possible and when necessary, she
helped out with available resources . . . her own and anyone else's
she could access.

Her confidence and persistence paved the way for many
BCHS students to rise far above their expected lot in life. Some
became educators, doctors, journalists, successful businessmen,
lawyers, and judges; there is a never-ending list. Still many more
achieved the priceless status of respected contributors to their
families and communities.

The quality of persevering in the face of limitations brings
great reward, both personal and public. For Mrs. Clemmer, it was
only what she expected from her "charges".

A Father, a Son . . . and Mrs. Clemmer

Edward Sneed

My son, David Sneed, was a sixteen year old sophomore in
high school around 1967. He decided that he wanted to quit
school. Since I knew Mrs. Clemmer was an administrator at the
school, I took him right on up to the school to have a visit. I hoped
this would straighten him up.

When we got to her office, I explained to Mrs. Clemmer the
situation that I was in with my son. I told her, "David thinks he
knows more than I do and that he could drop out and be just fine."

She continued to listen to me, and when I was finished, she
turned to David and said, "You think you know more than your
dad, don't you?"

He nodded and she proceeded, "Well, when you are twenty-one years old, you will be amazed at how much your daddy has learned in the next five years."

She went on with her sermon and we left. The next day, do you know where David was? He was right at school in his classes. He finished school and graduated in 1969. He found as he got older in life that Mrs. Clemmer's words were very valuable.

Mrs. Clemmer believed that words were very powerful and learning how to use words was about the best thing you could do.

- Paul Conn

More than a Grade

Valerie Hyberger Williams

Mrs. Clemmer was feared and respected by all who knew her. For two years, I hid from her for fear of doing something she didn't like or didn't think I should be doing. Imagine my dread and fear when I discovered that I had been placed in Mrs. Clemmer's Latin I class for my junior year. Then the most amazing thing happened.

The first day of Latin I, Mrs. Clemmer walked into the silent class. She closed the door and with that closure a transformation came. The hard, stern, assistant principal turned into the softest, most loving, and caring teacher I had ever witnessed.

From the first, I struggled with Latin. I spent hours at night trying to figure it out and, with the help of some loyal friends, managed to interpret a line or two of Mrs. Clemmer's favorite stories. Once I messed up horribly in front of the class.
I actually thought I was doing well. However, I read "once upon a time" when it should have been "at one time". She and the whole class laughed their heads off. Once I realized what I had done,
I did too.

Mrs. Clemmer never made you feel bad, even if you messed up. I have never felt more secure and safer in a class before or since. She did everything to help me but I'll confess I never learned Latin. When grade cards came out, I was ready to receive my "F" for
I knew I had failed.

When class was over, she called me up to her desk. She handed me my grade card and it had a "D" instead of the "F".

I looked at her in amazement and she smiled at me sweetly. I'll never forget her words. "Valerie, some people can do things better than others. It doesn't mean they don't try all the time. Latin isn't for everyone and you happen to be one of those people. If you hadn't come to class prepared everyday and tried your hardest, it would be different. Because you tried so hard, you haven't failed."

Only God and Mrs. Clemmer knew how I felt at that moment in time. I'm a teacher today because of her and have always kept her philosophy in mind when grade cards go out to my students. By the way, I don't teach Latin!

Valerie Hyberger Williams and Mrs. Clemmer 1998

When a student was really trying, but having limited success, Mrs. Clemmer would not demand more of that student than he could deliver.

- Sheridan Randolph

One Powerful Push

Stony Brooks

As a student at Bradley Central High School from 1960-1963, I did not realize Mrs. Clemmer knew who I was. Except for one small incident of my going down the "up" stairs, I rarely came in contact with her. However, just before graduation in 1963, she called me to her office --- which to any student was the "kiss of death".

She sat me down and asked me straight out what I was going to do after graduation. My reply was, "Mrs. Clemmer, I guess I'll just go over to one of the stove factories and get a job like most Clevelanders." Her response was "Stony, you can do better than that. What about college?"

I said, "Mrs. Clemmer, I am the first in my family to graduate from high school. Neither my family nor I can afford college."

She said, "If I could get you some scholarship money, would you go?" Hesitantly, I said, "Yes, I would give it a try". So, in a couple of days, she called me back to her office.

She said, "A local business has a $2,000 scholarship for you. Now get registered for college." So I did. Obviously $2,000 was not going to get me very far in college, but one thing she knew about me was that I was not a quitter and that I would not give up.

I finished my undergraduate work in four years with a natural science degree, majoring in math, physics, zoology, and chemistry. I then finished my graduate degree with honors in math and returned $1100 of the scholarship money to the donor.

I completed all of my college work without student loans. Later I chaired a committee of locals to create a scholarship to honor her at Cleveland State Community College.

> *She would find out what motivated you and then used it on you.*
>
> *- Jack Brown*

Maureen Olsson Lovelace

Coming to BCHS from a three room school in 1955 was culture shock! I was overwhelmed, not only by the size of Bradley, but also the reputation of the assistant principal, Mrs. Inez Clemmer. As if that wasn't frightening enough, Mrs. Clemmer was also the Latin I teacher.

For the first two weeks of that class, I remember crying because I was too afraid to ask for help. Finally, Mrs. Clemmer took matters into her own hands. She said she wanted to see me during my study hall period in her office. How I dreaded that!

When I reported to her office later that day, she put her work aside, closed the door, and, in a kind voice, said she was going to help me. All at once, with her assurance that I could master this course, the understanding dawned for me. For several days at the same time, I reported to her office, and she worked with me as if helping me were the only thing she had to do.

I'll never forget the valuable lessons learned from her. Probably the most important thing she taught me was perseverance in the face of difficulty. She followed my progress through my four years at BCHS and encouraged me to try out for a scholarship at UTC. I received that scholarship.

Maureen Lovelace, a Language Arts teacher at Ocoee Middle School, taught Latin to ninth graders when it was Bradley Junior High School.

Don Geren

In 1953, I started Bradley High School as a "know-it-all" freshman. After seven weeks, I decided to quit school, thinking I didn't need it because I wanted to make money *now*. I got a job and worked hard, but I soon discovered it wasn't as much fun as I thought it would be. I realized I would rather use my brain, so I started back to school as a freshman again.

At the beginning of my sophomore year, I had to take the placement tests. When the results came back, Mrs. Clemmer noticed my high scores and wanted to know why I was wasting my time (I was one of those good-boy, bad-boy students). She wanted me to settle down, get focused and prepare myself for college.

She asked me which college I was interested in. I told her that I didn't plan on going to college since my mother was making only $26 a week sewing at the Cleveland Woolen Mills. Mrs. Clemmer assured me that if I would apply myself and make good grades, she would provide me with the name of a gentleman who would sponsor me and lend me the money to get through college. For the first time in my life, Mrs. Clemmer had just provided me with a GOAL!!

I told her I would make a deal with her—I would work hard and make great grades and keep them great if she would agree to let me graduate with my original classmates. To do this, I would have to go to summer school and carry a full load, but I was willing! She worked it out and now I had a vision of being able to graduate in three years and go on to college with my original classmates.

I did graduate in 1957 with the classmates I had started out with as a freshman. I also was able to use a college loan program from Burlington Industries instead of getting money from the man Mrs. Clemmer provided. I went on to get my Master's Degree and have spent my adult life working at management positions and colleges.

I will always remember that Mrs. Clemmer believed in me and showed me that anything is possible if you have a desire to better yourself and are willing to work to make it happen.

Mildred Miller McGuire

Mrs. Clemmer was my Latin teacher for two years. She was a very hard taskmaster. She expected us to do our best. My best subject was not Latin, but rather was math. I later found out that math was also Mrs. Clemmer's favorite subject. She preferred teaching math.

She was never my math teacher. However, I won an East Tennessee Math contest in Algebra II. This fact got Mrs. Clemmer's attention. She called me into her office and explained to me that since I was good in math that I should be able to "win" a college scholarship. She handed me some large books and said, "You should study these this summer to perhaps improve your score on the other parts of the exam." These books were sample exams and included vocabulary typically on the scholarship exams.

I spent much of the summer lying on a quilt in my yard studying those books. Just as she predicted, when I took the exam I scored very high on the math part, but also did very well on the other parts and became a National Merit Commended Scholar.

I went to the University of Tennessee on scholarship and graduated in Engineering. Neither of my parents had finished the eighth grade. How very thankful I am that Mrs. Clemmer took the time and interest to inspire and change lives for the better.

CHAPTER 5

A WOMAN OF CARING

Caring: Showing understanding of others by treating them
with kindness, compassion, generosity, and a forgiving
spirit.

*Too often we underestimate the power of a touch, a smile,
a kind word... or the smallest act of caring, all of which
have the potential to turn a life around.*
- Leo F. Buscaglia

Tough, but Tender

She was a class act with a caring heart under that tough exterior.
- Brenda Beaty Remine

Perhaps an entire book could be written about the caring acts Inez Clemmer performed during her thirty year tenure as teacher and administrator at BCHS. Many of her deeds of kindness were unseen and undiscovered until the search for "Clemmer stories" began. No one expected the sheer number and varieties of such stories that took place through the years, and one can only wonder how many more still go untold.

Much irony lies in the fact that Mrs. Clemmer was so often initially viewed by students with a fear that commanded respect. Her "tough projects" may have continued to experience that reality. Many others, however, came to know the tender interior that not only discerned the struggles and neediness of some Bradley High students, but moved beyond the call of "duty" to ease those hardships.

Tender, *Not* Tough

Gaytha Bradley Ogle

My father was taken very ill one morning before I left for school. We thought he had suffered a stroke, but Mother sent me on to school as there was nothing I could do. Mrs. Clemmer called the hospital, the doctor, and my home during the day to find out about him for me. I was relieved when she came back to say he was at home. Her kindness and attention were so much appreciated then and fondly remembered even now.

She helped them to be a better person.

- Herbert Lackey

Marsha King Goodwin

I only attended BCHS in 1965, my freshman year. My mother passed away in January of that year and my father remarried, so we moved back to Chattanooga.

I remember Mrs. Clemmer being so sympathetic and kind to me. I never had her in class and, like the multitudes, was terrified of her. I remember her calling me to her office, thinking I had violated some rule. I was very shy at that time and was so relieved that she merely wanted to extend her condolences.

Skip forward thirty years to 1996. I was the first Middle School Teacher of the Year for the Inez Clemmer award. She was there and congratulated each of us. She spoke to me and said that she did remember my attending one year and that my mother had passed away. I was so stunned that she would remember me and that the year 1965 was a particularly tragic one for me. It made an indelible impression.

Brenda Evans

In 1962, I stayed home from school because I was sick. Mrs. Clemmer called to check on me. I told her I was sick and would return to school when I was better.

Later that same afternoon, Mrs. Clemmer called my house and talked to my grandmother because I was sleeping. Mrs. Clemmer told my grandmother that she was not calling to check up on me, but wanted to make sure I was okay and not home by myself.

Robert D. "Bob" Burris

I was Mrs. Clemmer's newspaper delivery boy. My mother had a nervous condition and would occasionally make me stay home with her during the school day. I would then deliver Mrs. Clemmer's paper and I was embarrassed that I had to stay out of school and then deliver her newspaper.

She was always nice about it. Of course, she checked the situation out with relatives. Once she knew the circumstances were legitimate, she always understood and did not embarrass me.

Marty Fulbright Semmes

It was 1954 and Latin I class. This ole gal took off her sock and shoe and put her foot on Mrs. Clemmer's desk. Some larger girl had stepped on my big toe and, I believe, broke it. Mrs. Clemmer gave me the sympathy and love my big toe needed.

Anderson "Jute" Miller

One school day, Mrs. Clemmer and I were looking out the window, and we saw a special guy with a handicap carrying books for another student that had broken his leg. Mrs. Clemmer had tears in her eyes. She understood problems and people of all kinds.

Patsy Coker Smith

Somehow or other Mrs. Clemmer became aware that I was a Bachman Home student and she was so kind to me. She was supportive, even asking me to sit in on her Latin II class. This helped me a lot and I saw the soft, caring side of a marvelous educator who was truly concerned for others.

Peggy Turner Allen

I had a good friend named Zelda. Zelda came from a really poor family. One day Mrs. Clemmer came to me to ask about Zelda and told me that if she ever needed anything to please tell her. Until that day, I hadn't thought one way or another about Mrs. Clemmer, but after that day I had a whole new respect for her.

Dick Pelley

It was January 13, 1959 during my junior year. Mrs. Clemmer came and got me out of Mrs. Fitzgerald's fourth period English class. She took me into her office and told me that my father had died. The compassion that she displayed has been etched in my memory all these years.

She got Billy Collins and David Howard to drive me home because I lived in Calhoun and had to hitchhike to Bradley each day. She also came to the receiving of friends.

As a professor of Psychology at Tennessee Wesleyan College, I have attended many funerals, weddings, and birth experiences in my thirty-five years in education thanks to the heartwarming model of Mrs. Clemmer.

Her sternness when handling situations that arose always kept us on our toes, but the end result always revealed to us how much she really cared for each student she encountered.
- Carolyn Ferguson

Say Cheese!

Rachel Nunley Pickett

Even though I wasn't in Mrs. Clemmer's classroom, I feel like I owe her half my life. Thanks to her, I have a good job (the same one I've had since graduation in 1962). I also owe her my smile since she was the one responsible for all of my dental work getting started.

I was sure that my teeth were past helping. Mrs. Clemmer helped me both emotionally and materially. I now know the importance of good dental hygiene in early years. I have tried to teach my girls this and I hope that someday I will be able to help others financially who might be in the condition I was then.

Secret Service

Janice Crye Suits

My mom worked with Lee Clemmer at Magic Chef for many years, and she had remained friends with him after she was stricken with multiple sclerosis. Since I had never met Mr. and Mrs. Clemmer, I did not know all the connections I would have with them throughout my life, and how they worked behind the scenes to make my future possible.

As an upperclassman, I worked in the principal's office and did errands for Mr. Schultz and Mrs. Clemmer. I was one of the few girls who wanted to go to college. Most of them wanted to get married and be housewives or secretaries. I had no real beau at that time and I was very independent due to my mom's illness and Mrs. Clemmer's influence in my life.

Money was an issue for my college attendance, but little did I know that God had provided an angel in the form of Mrs.

Clemmer to allow me to attend Tennessee Wesleyan College. She gave recommendations for me to have scholarships through Magic Chef, the American Legion, and the Dollars for Scholars program. Her brother, M.L. Smith, also helped me obtain an academic scholarship.

I never knew of many of these wonderful deeds that the Clemmers carried out for me until I had my own classroom.

I'm telling you, it's awful. Here it is just two weeks to graduation and we have senior girls who don't even have plans to get married. Mrs. Clemmer to Sheridan Randolph

Dennis Spurlin

My dad and uncles lived next door to Mrs. Clemmer when they were boys. The Spurlin boys cared for her yard for fifteen years. While she was at school she was known as a disciplinarian, school teacher, and vice-principal, but around the neighborhood she as known as a kindhearted lady. At times, she gave Little Debbies and colas to all the neighborhood kids.

Vesta Guthrie Jones

I was at Bradley from 1964 to 1968. I was an office aide for Mrs. Clemmer in my junior year. Because I was never absent, I had no reason to be considered for Mrs. Clemmer's "watch closely" list. From the first she trusted me.

> *She was a disciplinarian, there's no doubt about that. But, she had the softest heart in the world.*
> *- Bill Schultz*

One day she sent me for her billfold. She was going to give me money to pay for something that my family couldn't afford. She had asked me to get the money out which she had hidden in a special pocket. I told her it wasn't there. I was so naïve that I didn't know there were pockets, but I brought her the billfold before class and she gave me the money.

Later, Mrs. Clemmer matched me up with a group at one of the churches in the area. They paid for my lunch in the cafeteria and bought me an outfit. I was able to meet a few interesting people through this arrangement.

She gave away a big, big part of her salary every year for any student that was in need of a dress for prom or to get that haircut she said they needed.

- Bill Schultz

Tireless Tutor

Leslie Smith Christian

Inez Clemmer was my great aunt on my father's side of the family. Both of my grandmothers had passed away when I was very young, so she basically was my grandmother. Her home was located just up the street from my house, so we could ride our bikes up the street to visit her and my Uncle Lee on a daily basis.

When I was in the ninth grade, I struggled on a continual basis in math, specifically algebra. My grades were not acceptable to my parents so Aunt Inez began to tutor me four nights a week. What always amazed me was that, at the time, she was 76 years old! She was sharp as a tack and her knowledge of the subject was extraordinary.

For two years, she managed to find enough patience to pull me up from making D's to making B's in both Algebra I and II.

Now that I'm older, I can see she was only interested in what was best for me.

- Evelyn McCurry

CHAPTER 6

A WOMAN OF
SELF-DISCIPLINE

**Self-Discipline: Demonstrating hard work. Controlling
your emotions, words, actions, impulses, and desires.**

*We all have dreams. But in order to make dreams into
reality, it takes an awful lot of determination, dedication,
self-discipline, and effort.*

- Jesse Owens

NO EXCUSES

With an amused twinkle in her eyes, she would smile and say,
"Okay now, that was nice, but let's get right back to work."
We always did.

- Nora Varnell Hilburn

Inez Clemmer lived in a generation that possessed a powerful work ethic. She modeled it and she demanded it both in the classroom and in extracurricular settings. The effort itself was more important than the success of the effort.

She also understood the importance of the ability to discipline one's behavior and emotions. That strength would be crucial in controlling the impulsiveness and immaturity that so often sent teenagers down dangerous and unproductive paths.

"Self" discipline would be the key in producing gifted athletes, successful students, and good citizens. It would be their motivating factor in dreaming big, building a better future, and in overcoming a difficult past. Mrs. Clemmer understood the potential for a disciplined life. She motivated and encouraged Bradley High students to value it also.

Lessons in Latin?

Doris Ann Webb Wright

Mrs. Clemmer taught Latin and algebra. She had three classes. Class began as soon as she entered the room and slammed the door behind her. She began class with a question. There was no sleeping in her class. She didn't give much homework, but she expected you to have it. She would ask a student to come up front to answer, but she never made a student feel stupid.

Vesta Guthrie Jones

I was a student in Mrs. Clemmer's Latin II class. She demanded excellence from her students, just like she did from herself. The class was routinely assigned a translation each week. We were expected to recite it each time. Most of us did not expect to be called on, so we would not study like we should have.

However, when we started a unit on Julius Caesar, she assigned each of us just one paragraph. Our individual work on this section of translation was the best ever.

Janice Crye Suits

As a sophomore at Bradley, I met Mrs. Clemmer for the first time while registering for classes. I remember there were two teachers who were teaching Latin. One line was very long; these students were waiting to sign up for the other teacher.

Since the line was short for Mrs. Clemmer's class, I got in that line. After I met Mrs. Clemmer and enlisted in her class, several students came up to ask me if I was CRAZY! They indicated that she was the assistant principal.

I have never regretted my decision to get in the shorter line. Mrs. Clemmer taught me more about history, Latin, and life than anyone else ever had before in school. As she told of Greek and Roman history, we became true classical students. Julius and Augustus Caesar became real people to us and the conquering of Gaul and the Britons were acts right out of Action comic books. Not only did we extend our vocabulary through the study of Latin derivatives, but we learned how to become successful teachers through her example.

She was among the first to make me realize that learning, just for its own sake, was a great value.

- Ann Almond Pope

Patsy Coker Smith

I had Mrs. Clemmer for Latin II my sophomore year of high school. Her classroom was very much under control. I had been forewarned that I would be unprepared for her classroom. She was known to be a very strict, hard teacher.

Well, her classroom certainly lived up to its reputation. No one, I mean no one missed her scrutiny. She would call on you and you answered or else. There was no shrugging shoulders, or "I don't know."

There happened to be another student in my class whose name was Patricia Cofer. My maiden name is Patsy Coker and

Mrs. Clemmer called me Patricia Coker. She just assumed that my name was Patricia since I was called Patsy. I could never tell the difference in the two names when she called them.

Mrs. Clemmer always received respect, obedience, and your quick attention.

- Glenda Bryant Kyker

Gail Kerr Kearns

Mrs. Clemmer used her classes to talk informally about books and about the ideas she had found within them. I remember at the beginning of each year, she gave us our choice of textbooks for the class. If we picked out copy from the shiny pile of new books, we had to return them in pristine condition at the end of the year. But if we picked them from the raggedy pile, destined to be thrown out, we could keep them and mark in them as we pleased. Many of us did just that and still have our old books to this day.

If I were to try now to characterize those enriched classes of so many years ago, I would say that Mrs. Clemmer was teaching us not so much Latin, but conscious habits of mind employed by the literate and educated adult of any age, time and place. Under her tutelage, we learned to delight in the disciplines of reading, thinking, and learning for its own sake.

Chris Rodie

I was a member of the graduating class of 1966 and a student of Mrs. Clemmer in Latin. I was a member of what I believe was the only Latin III class ever taught at Bradley. Several members of my class – led, I believe by Cissy Tidwell— petitioned Mrs. Clemmer to offer the class. We were all delighted when she agreed to do so. Needless to say, the class was rigorous. We had, among other things, to translate Cicero from sight with no notes!

One of Mrs. Clemmer's favorite class experiences over the years was teaching a third-year Latin class by popular demand.

- Nancy Carney, Cleveland Daily Banner

Boys Under Control

Nora Varnell Hilburn

I will never forget my first day in Mrs. Clemmer's
Algebra I class. While waiting for class to begin, I looked around
the room and thought, "This class will be a disaster." By some
stroke of bad luck, at least five of the most disruptive boys I had
been in classes with over the years were all in one class. My first
thought was that Mrs. Clemmer would be a nervous wreck before
the week was out, and none of us would learn anything all year
because discipline would be impossible.

Of course, I did not know Inez Clemmer. She managed
to bring out the best in all of us. Even the boys, who had driven
many teachers to tears, worked hard and surprised everybody with
their intelligence, wit, and ability to behave and learn. When at
times their funny remarks would be made, she always laughed
as much as any of us. Then, with an amused twinkle in her eyes,
she would smile at the young man of the moment and say, "Okay,
that was nice, but let's get back to work". We always did.

*When Mrs. Clemmer spoke you listened to every word, and then
did exactly what you were told.*

- Tom Johnson

The Ocoeean, 1949

Pay Off

Bernie Orr, M.D.

Mrs. Clemmer continually encouraged her students to develop good study habits to pave their way for college. She even nurtured a sense of competitiveness as a motivational tool. In my case, the encouragement and challenge took hold.

Although my family was very limited financially, I received assistance from the Rymer foundation and eventually attended school in Memphis where I graduated with my medical degree!

Oddly enough, I was also taught in fourth grade at Mayfield School by Mrs. Clemmer's sister. It was her instruction that enabled me to finally master my multiplication tables.

I had some good teachers, but Mrs. Clemmer was my all time favorite. You can quote me on that.

- Oney Dodd Hambright

Housekeeping Matters

Rebecca Hysinger Goins

Mrs. Clemmer's long arm of expectation definitely extended to the BCHS majorette squad. The school allowed the use of a room for their clothing and practice items. However, Becky remembers the frequent admonition to "keep this room in order", accompanied by the assurance that failure to do so would result in the loss of the room.

The natural result of this was the scurrying around and straightening in anticipation of Mrs. Clemmer's arrival and room check.

George Nerren

During my senior year, a stone wall was built along the walkway between the gym and the auditorium. I couldn't resist writing my name in the wet concrete. It didn't take Mrs. Clemmer long to call me to the office. She didn't ask me if I did it, she just said, "Well, George what are you going to do about you name written in the concrete?"

I replied that I intended to learn how to mix concrete and repair the damage. She said, "I hope you learned something from this, at least how to mix concrete." For me, this was a life lesson about self-discipline and being responsible for actions.

Yes, after Mrs. Clemmer, even army boot camp was tolerable.
- Sheridan Randolph

"Self" Control

Mary Manges Reeves

As a junior and senior, I worked as Mrs. Clemmer's office assistant one hour every school day. One day, an irate parent came to see her during my work period. This parent called her every name in the book and then some.

Mrs. Clemmer was gracious, but firm. When the parent left, she turned to me with tears in her eyes and said, "Sometimes, Mary, you just have to let people vent as
long and hard as they want." That has been forty-two years ago, and I remember as if it were yesterday. It made me realize this wonderful, powerful lady was so truly human with feelings just like us all, but with an innate strength of restraint and endurance.

But I can say this, she really did help my education because there were times when I didn't feel like going but I got up and went to school anyway because I didn't want to face Mrs. Clemmer the next day.
- Denny Williams

CHAPTER 7

A WOMAN OF CITIZENSHIP

Citizenship: Being law abiding and involved in service to school, community, and country.

The true test of civilization is not the census, not the size of the cities...no, but the kind of man the country turns out.

- Ralph Waldo Emerson

STUDENT COUNCIL

Dolores Moore, *President;* Tommy Newman, *Vice-President;* Barbara Benton, *Secretary;* Clyde Kyle, *Treasurer;* Mrs. Lee Clemmer and Mrs. Raulston, *Sponsors;* Bill Bacon, David Jones, Betty Higgins, Richard Carroll, Bill Hargis, T. Roy Jones, and Aileen Young.

The Ocoeean 1952

Student Council Motto 1952

The purpose of this organization shall be to train for good citizenship along democratic lines, maintain a high standard of truth, honor, and duty, promote a happier school life, and foster a feeling of loyalty among students and teachers.

Let Freedom Ring

I am convinced that if every judgeship, at every level, were filled with a "Mrs. Clemmer", the benefits to society would be immeasurable.

- Judge Andrew F. Bennett, Jr.

"If Cleveland, Tennessee had a Statue of Liberty, it would have Mrs. Clemmer's face". This comment was made at an appreciation banquet for Inez Clemmer. For sure, Mrs. Clemmer cherished the ideal of citizenship and all that accompanied it. As one story will indicate, she even sacrificed her job security for the freedom to vote without duress. Although Commissioner Mitchell Lyle once presented her with a "get out of jail free" letter, there was little chance it would have ever been redeemed.

So what did her citizenship zeal mean to students at Bradley High School? As usual, if Mrs. Clemmer believed it, she lived it. She also expected the same adherence to the tenets of citizenship from the students under her authority. They should both obey the law of the land and learn to follow school rules. They would become productive contributors or answer to her, at least while they were high school students.

Perhaps more than the others, this trait of citizenship actually combines all of the other character qualities. They would all be reflected in a person of outstanding citizenship; a person like Inez Clemmer.

Voting and Visiting

Walter Presswood

When I was running for school board, Mrs. Clemmer sent word that she wanted to see me. I had heard a lot of stories about Mrs. Clemmer. I went to her house with some trepidation in my heart, not really knowing what to expect. She didn't want to do anything but encourage me.

She wanted to sign my petition, but she wanted me to bring it to her. So, I did drop by for that purpose. We had talked for a while and she had not said much about the school board.

We talked about friends in Benton and issues in Bradley County schools. Then she signed my petition and wished me well. Every time from that point on when I ran, I went to visit Mrs. Clemmer. It usually took about an hour or longer, but it was always a delightful visit.

A Matter of Conscience

Don Smith

For a while after they married, Aunt Inez and Uncle Lee lived in Benton where Aunt Inez taught at Polk County High School. Before that she had taught and, I think, coached the girls' basketball team at Ducktown High School.

One day not too long after they married, Aunt Inez had a meeting with the Polk County sheriff, who at that time was the dominant figure in Polk County politics. He told her that he expected all persons who worked for Polk County in any way to vote his ticket in the coming elections.

I doubt that he thought she would give him any trouble. My mother and Aunt Inez's first cousin had grown up together. Now this cousin was married to the sheriff's son. I think that the sheriff probably thought that she would go along with his expectation. It was, moreover, the great economic depression of the 1930's; consequently, many people were without work, and those with work were glad to have it.

In spite of all of this, Aunt Inez told the sheriff that the ballot is secret and that she would not tell him for whom she planned to vote. As a citizen she had the right to vote for the candidates of her choice, and she planned to exercise that right. Whereupon he told her that she had better look for a teaching position elsewhere.

And so Aunt Inez lost her teaching position in Polk County because she defended her right to vote freely. She and Uncle Lee moved to Bradley County when she obtained a position teaching at Bradley High School. This was, I believe in 1937 or 1938.

I never heard Aunt Inez express any bitterness or anger about losing her position in Polk County. She treated the entire affair as simply a matter of standing up for her rights as a citizen.

My husband and I don't agree on which presidential candidate to support. I think I'll get one bumper sticker for my side of the car and he can put his on his side of the car.

- Inez Clemmer to Sheridan Randolph

Clothing Wars

Don Bivens

I remember one incident that was a good example of Mrs. Clemmer's teaching us through her actions. Our concert band was scheduled to leave after morning classes for a trip to a band festival. Some of our female band members decided it would be more comfortable to travel in the bus wearing pants rather than dresses. This was probably correct in terms of comfort, but in 1957 the school dress code did not permit female students to wear pants to school.

Shortly after the first period classes began, Mrs. Clemmer announced on the intercom that certain people had come to school with improper clothing and they should report to her office. Mrs. Clemmer required each of the students to go home and return in clothing consistent with the dress code.

Although there were comments made about this being a minor infraction of school rules, we definitely received the message that Mrs. Clemmer expected everyone to follow the school rules. The fact that I still remember this incident after forty-nine years is a good example of Mrs. Clemmer teaching us through her high standards and expectations.

Kathy Murray Morelock

During my junior year, I worked as Mrs. Clemmer's student assistant first period. She managed the attendance as well as some discipline. I cannot remember how I wound up in that position, but it allowed me free reign to roam the halls delivering messages to unsuspecting students and informing him or her that, "Mrs. Clemmer needs to see you in the office."

We were also dealing with dress code issues thirty plus years ago. . . I remember that girls could not wear pants (of any kind), yet the height of fashion was wearing the shortest mini skirts along with fish net hose. I do not remember Mrs. Clemmer specifically *saying* anything about my short skirts, but I do recall several occasions where she would take a "loooong" look and perhaps slightly touch the hem . . .

My great aunt remembers that if you wore a dress that was too short, Mrs. Clemmer would make you go home and change clothes.
- Betty Melton Gamble, as told to Katie Melton.

Cleveland . . . and Beyond

Linda Elkins Moore

Since high school graduation, I held the same job. I was employed with Claude H. Climer, the Bradley County Clerk. It was the one Mrs. Clemmer recommended me for in May of 1965.

At age 17, I was graduating from Bradley High and financially unable to attend college. Of all the qualified students, it remains a mystery why I was recommended. But, I tried especially hard to make Mr. Climer a good employee because of the confidence Mrs. Clemmer had in my ability.

Jack Brown

Jack Brown left BCHS in 1950 to join the Army. He indicates that his 20 year military career took him to many places. One recollection includes going to the Arctic Circle, whereupon he happened to meet a former classmate.

The classmate's first question was, "When have you been home?" The second question was, "Is Mrs. Clemmer still at Bradley High?" The third question asked, "How is she?"

It was always that way, wherever he went. Mrs. Clemmer was invariably a topic of conversation when her former students met. Brown, who ranks himself as one of Mrs. Clemmer's "mischievous" students, believes there is "no one else in Bradley County who has touched as many lives". He was thankful that she "looked past the mischief and on down the road".

How far-reaching your influence continues to be! I taught reading in public schools. We were in Montana for thirteen years. Children there know you now. We were in Mississippi seven years and in North Carolina seven years. If I've had a class, they've heard of you.

- Linda Mital McConnell

In Spite of Themselves

Sheridan Randolph

If called upon to name a local person who could be considered "great", most of us would initially retort, "there is none." Then, upon some reflection, we would begin to think of good citizens who have made their respective contributions to the betterment of the community. The list of names would be long. However, when we begin to focus on whose life has influenced so many others lives for good and whose name is spoken in awe and reverence by people who have not seen her in over twenty years, the name of Inez Clemmer comes to mind.

I believe that Mrs. Clemmer, more than anyone else around her, realized the value of education and gave her undivided efforts toward educating young people whether they thought they wanted to be educated or not. She knew that education was the way to economic opportunity, improved self-esteem, and a better quality of life in general.

I had a lot of friends that went through the Bradley County School system. Even to this day, they say how appreciative they are for the way she demanded them to be the best they could be, and how she really pushed them to learn and taught them how to learn and study and to be prepared to be successful, and to be good citizens and good students.

- Steve Ratterman

Seeing the kind of citizens some of us have become, you may not want to claim any responsibility for what we are. Still, the worst of us are better than we would have been without your influence.

- Andrew Bennett, Jr.

Guarding her Turf

Dennis Spurlin

Rumor has it that once the neighborhood boys were out water ballooning cars at night as they went down the street. Mrs. Clemmer heard the boys outside, turned on her porch light, and came outside.

The boys scattered as Mrs. Clemmer came out and confiscated the water balloons. The next day she approached the boys, knowing it was them the night before. She asked them if they knew which "outside" boys had water ballooned the cars the night before because she knew that none of her boys would do such a thing!

Needless to say, there was no more water ballooning from the neighborhood boys.

Paying Her Way

Peggy Johnson

In 1985, several people at Broad Street United Methodist Church decided to honor Mrs. Clemmer with an appreciation banquet. The committee was composed of Connie Day, Tom Johnson, Stony Brooks, myself, and Jack Brown, who was a member of First Cumberland Presbyterian.

I worked at Merchants Bank. A few days before the banquet, Mrs. Clemmer walked up to my window and said, "I understand you may have some tickets for the dinner at BCHS on March 8."

I replied, "Yes, Ma'am."

She said, "I want to purchase two, please."

What a lady . . . she bought her tickets to the dinner in her honor!

Mrs. Clemmer loved God, her family, her school, her students, and her country.

- Jerry Frazier

Inez Clemmer Appreciation Banquet, March 8, 1985

Inez Clemmer and nephew Gary Smith

Inez Clemmer with great-niece Leslie Smith Christian
and Mary Passavant

Because we are grateful to you for...

M any years of loyal service to Bradley High School,

R eminding us of the importance of our religious, educational and social life,

S omehow, making us believe in ourselves,

C are and concern for our welfare,

L eaving us with more than a knowledge of Latin and algebra,

E ncouragement when we were deeply depressed,

M aking us stop and think before we jumped,

M emorable service as sponsor of the Student Council,

E ndeavoring to guide us, without dominating us, and

R ecognizing and understanding our needs,

We, the Class of 1954, do dedicate to you...
Mrs. Clemmer, our Ocoeean.

CHAPTER 8

A WOMAN OF HONESTY

Honesty: Telling the truth, admitting wrongdoing. Being trustworthy and acting with integrity.

No legacy is so rich as honesty.

- William Shakespeare

Truth or Consequences

Stop right there. Go back to the beginning, and this time I want to hear the truth.

                                    - Mrs. Clemmer
                              to a student in her office,
                          as overheard by Eugenia Rodgers.

There were a couple of exceptional abilities that students and faculty invariably noted about Inez Clemmer. One was her uncanny ability to be everywhere at once. The other, as these stories will relate, was her almost infallible talent at sniffing out a lie. Years later, former students and staff still remember her skill at uncovering falsehoods.

Honesty was a non-negotiable for Mrs. Clemmer. She respected it in others and expected it from everyone. Being truthful from the start was certainly a student's best and wisest option. If consequences were forthcoming, they had better be for the deed in question and not for lying to Mrs. Clemmer.

Even more notable, as one story will show, Mrs. Clemmer trained others in her refined art of discerning lies and truth. The result was a host of "mini-Clemmers" on a mission to unmask culprits who added dishonesty to their list of crimes.

Truth Tracker

Debbie Humberd Kimsey

Being one of Mrs. Clemmer's office aides afforded me the opportunity to learn many things from her tutelage. Not only did she command respect, responsibility and honesty from me, she expected it from others. One of the best things she taught me, however, was the fine art of lying, or rather how to deduce who was and who wasn't lying. As trained mini-wardens, we were given coursework in how to separate the fakers from the non-fakers, the lies from the fibs, and the reality from the truth. During the last periods of the day, we had to have two aides to handle the influx of students attempting to leave early, while Mrs. Clemmer scurried back and forth guarding the hallways, back entrances, and parking lots.

You see, when Mrs. Clemmer was out of the office, we were in charge. We checked on absentee students, wrote excuses for tardiness, and had to make the decision as to whether a student could leave campus early or not for doctor appointments, family trips, funerals, or whatever. We quickly learned, therefore, to determine who was telling the truth and who wasn't. I must have learned my warden lessons well, though, as some of the students *finally* learned. When Martha Clevenger or Maureen Poole would come to the office and see me sitting there, they would just turn around and leave. Believe me; we needed a revolving door for some of them.

Testing, Testing

Connie Day

I remember Miss. Lucy Turner and her Latin class. A boy in her class stole her final exam and passed it around to all of us --- we all passed the test, but our joy was short-lived when Mrs. Clemmer found out about it. She came into class the next day and asked us all to clear off our desks and get out one sheet of paper and a pencil --- THEN we each had to write our confession. As I remember, I was less than honest on my first try as was Brenda McLain. We felt so guilty that we went to the office later and made a full confession. Mrs. Clemmer was tough and no one could put anything over   on her, but she was always fair. She was always consistent.

Milteen Hornsby Cartwright

Something very special that I recall about being in Mrs. Clemmer's class was no one cheated --- not even those who cheated in other classes. She could (and did) leave the classroom during key difficult exams and no one would cheat.

When I was in her presence, I could have never told her a fib.
- Herbert Lackey

Gotcha!

Eugenia Rodgers

Eugenia Rodgers, BCHS teacher from 1938-1977 remembers watching Mrs. Clemmer "whip through" the lineup outside her door one morning.

A young man standing in front of Mrs. Clemmer's desk was obviously there for the first time. That was obvious because he was rattling off one excuse after another. Frequent visitors knew better.

When he paused, Mrs. Clemmer held up her hand and said, "Stop right there, go back to the beginning, and this time I want to hear the truth."

He (gulp) did and she did.

And that's all there was to that.

She could look into your eyes and always seemed to know if you were telling the truth.

- Eddie Cartwright

Gerdline Mull

My grandmother remembers that she told the bus driver to let her and some friends off at the Village Mall. The next day Mrs. Clemmer called her into her office and asked, "Gerdile, what did you do yesterday?" She told her and was given detention.

- As told to Brook Hines

When asked if it was true that he had said he could "never lie" to Mrs. Clemmer, Cunnyngham said, "That's true. I never could." -
- Nancy Carney, Cleveland Daily Banner

A "Deer" Story

Vernon "Clem" Fannin

It was the day before opening day of the deer hunting season and the hunting camp needed an advanced party to go early and set up camp. I was feeling a little sick (staying in school) that Friday afternoon, so I checked out "sick" and headed for the mountains.

After a weekend of unsuccessful hunting, I returned to school Monday with my "he was sick Friday" note written for me by a friend at the bus stop. Between classes, who but Mrs. Clemmer stopped me in the hall. "How did you do hunting?" asked Mrs. C.

After picking my chin up from the floor, I replied, "Not good."

She said she had checked my grades and I was free to go hunting anytime I wanted. "BUT DON'T YOU EVER LIE TO ME AGAIN." Message received loud and clear.

After a week of detention, we never had a problem.

Who Fooled Who?

Don Akins

One beautiful spring day I thought I would take a day off from school and enjoy the wonderful weather. Well, knowing that Mrs. Clemmer's routine for following up on absentees was a phone call, I decided to call her first, so that I would be free to go and do whatever I wanted to do the rest of the day.

Upon reaching her, I proceeded to tell her how sick I was and couldn't bring myself to come to school that day. (I thought I got one ahead of her.) So, Mrs. Clemmer proceeded to tell me that she knew I was not a student to lie about being sick and miss school.

That's all it took to spoil my plans. That day was very miserable and long. I couldn't enjoy my day off and couldn't wait to get to school the next day.

Finding Favor

George Nerren

During my sophomore year at BCHS, I was a student in Mrs. Clemmer's Latin II class. She was an extraordinary teacher with high academic standards and expectations. To this day,

I don't know how she managed to teach Latin classes and perform her duties as assistant principal, but she did an exceptional job in both areas.

At the end of the first semester, the grade on my report card was much higher than I expected it to be. So I told Mrs. Clemmer that she must have made a mistake in averaging my grades. She discovered that she had miscalculated my grade and adjusted it. Seated at her desk, she glanced up at me with eyes looking over the top of her glasses and said, "George, you have restored my faith in humanity."

It was a great lesson in honesty. To this day, I remember the feeling that I had done something worthy of her commendation. It meant a lot to me then and does even today. (It also helped me on several occasions later when I was referred to her office for disciplinary matters.)

True Confession

Janice Crye Suits

One day I arrived early to school and was in the restroom when a student from Bachman Home came up to me and asked if I would give her a ride to the bus station to go see her mother in Sevierville. I felt sorry for her and I took her to the Trailways Station in downtown Cleveland.

I arrived back at school in time to make first period class and I thought I had done the right thing. After second period, I was called to Mrs.Clemmer's office. I knew that for some reason I must have done something wrong.

As I was standing in front of her, she asked me if I had taken the girl to the bus station. I responded with a "No", and she said I could go. But respecting Mrs. Clemmer as I did, I pivoted and cried that I had taken the girl to the bus station. Mrs. Clemmer explained to me that the situation the girl was returning to was not one that would be suitable for her.

Of course, I was sorry and I have always regretted fibbing to Mrs. Clemmer. But, in her own special way, she comforted me, and I left her office feeling fine and forgiven.

Reverse Honesty, Clemmer Style

Jeannie Callaway Crocco

I just barely squeaked by in math. A "D" was cause for celebration. Mrs. Clemmer would hand my papers back and always say, "You are such an underachiever, when will you start using your brain?"

Many moons, much later, I finally found that brain and made Honors when I completed my Masters Degree. However, I never got to tell her.

- Yearbook Dedication Presentation 1969

CHAPTER 9

A WOMAN OF COURAGE

Courage: Doing the right thing in the face of difficulty and following your conscience instead of the crowd.

Courage is what it takes to stand up and speak: courage is also what it takes to sit down and listen.

- author unknown

Great Expectations

I learned early on from her the importance of doing the right thing regardless of the consequences.

- Don Smith,
nephew of Inez Clemmer

Courage may seem an odd topic to address in the everydayness of life, especially on a school campus. For sure, it would be demanded in certain professions more than others, such as that of a soldier, firefighter, or police officer. But how so for students and teachers?

The truth is, living with character takes courage. It takes courage to make right choices when the wrong way seems easier. Courage is required to walk away from negative peer pressure and live differently. Defending the helpless may call for courage. Speaking up when it wouldn't be popular requires courage. Sometimes it may even take courage to come to school.

When Mrs. Clemmer taught at Bradley High School, guns, knives, and deadly violence were seldom encountered. It was facing Mrs. Clemmer that often took courage. Facing the consequences for breaking the rules --- that took courage!

But Mrs. Clemmer had her own brand of courage. She had the courage to do what was right and to demand what was right even if it meant she wouldn't be liked or understood. Oddly enough, time has erased those negatives. Even students who found nothing to like about this strict educator at the time, now recognize and respect the motives and results of her firmness.

Praying For Courage

Bill McClure

It was during my sophomore year of high school and I had been out of school for two days with the flu. Mother and Dad were both at work and I was home alone when the phone rang. When I answered, this lady on the other end asked, "Bill, how are you feeling?"

I said, "Oh fine. I'm just "laying out" of school for a couple of days."

The lady then said, "Well, this is Mrs. Clemmer and I thought I would just check to see how you were doing." I almost died right on the spot. I then tried to explain that I didn't really mean I was 'laying out' of school and that I was really sick, but I got little conversation from the other end of the phone.

I don't think I slept a wink that night. When I gave Mrs. Clemmer the note from my mom the next morning and she wrote out my white excuse, I believe I saw a faint smile on her lips.

Brenda Simmons McLain

One of the many things that I admired most about Mrs. Clemmer during my years at Bradley was the fact that she was in a position of power and that she handled it well. For quite a while, I felt fearful in her presence, but that fear was dispelled one day in her office.

Judy Bennett and I had spent days working up the nerve to ask if we could leave school early one Friday to go to a UT party with boyfriends. We took turns trying to push each other through the door first, and finally, side by side, made our request.

After she explained the importance of being in school, and the triviality of such parties, she looked us in the eye, smiled, and said, "Of course, I couldn't stop you if you just left. All I could do would be to give you a couple of hours of detention."

It was an easy price to pay. We knew it, and I know that she did too.

Mrs. Clemmer was a force to be reckoned with.
- Alice Rogers

Joe Hamilton

My dad, J. Paul Hamilton, came to Bradley Central High in 1946 from Valley Head School, a small country school near the present day Valley Head United Methodist Church on Mouse Creek Road. The youngest of 12 children born to Albert Henry and Gracie Mae (Griffin) Hamilton, J. Paul quickly became known as one of the class clowns, much more interested in football, girls, and generally having a good time than in his studies. In short, Mrs. Inez Clemmer came to know the young jokester J. Paul quite well.

Because of their frequent encounters and the stories I had heard, by the time I got to Bradley, I was so scared of Mrs. Clemmer that I almost threw up when I was called to her office one of the first days of my freshman year. As I stood in front of her desk, I tried to think of what I could have possibly done wrong.

Mrs. Clemmer looked at me with those black eyes and said, "Joe, I remember your father and I am well pleased to see the man he has grown to be, especially that he has chosen to run for election as a County Court member. As far as YOUR behavior and study habits are concerned, I do hope you have taken after your mother."

Mrs. Inez Clemmer never had a problem with me.

Steve Gibson

Probably the most memorable experience I had with Mrs. Clemmer took place one summer day when I was mowing her yard. Evidently I was trying to hurry so I could get to the golf course, and I got the lawnmower too close to her doormat that was on the sidewalk. The lawnmower blade made it look like a jigsaw puzzle.

Finally, I got enough courage to knock on the door, ready to accept whatever punishment she would give, but to my delight she was one of the kindest persons I had ever known.

I can still hear her say, "Why, Steve, that 'ole mat needs to be replaced anyway!"

Carolyn Lacy Goins

Mrs. Goins had Mrs. Clemmer for Latin, but she was sent to her office once for talking in another class. Mrs. Clemmer made her wait until everyone else was gone. She thought she was dead.

Mrs. Clemmer told her that she knew better than to act like that. She also made her apologize to the other teacher.

- as told to Harry McMahan

Telling on Dad

Sheridan Randolph

When I was at Bradley High School, the only courses Mrs. Clemmer taught were Latin I and II, and since the majority of students did not elect either of those courses, they knew her only as a vice-principal. In this role, she was very much in evidence, handling most of the discipline.

How well I remember the terror in our hearts when we heard her voice say over the loud speaker, "Would the following please come to my office?" Even the innocent quaked.

It was not just the students who feared her, however. Frequently I arrived to school five to ten minutes late. Of course, this meant a trip to see Mrs. Clemmer each time. She informed me that I must stop being late.

I told her that I was always ready to come to school in time to get there, but it was my father who was making me late. She said, "I had that situation once before with a little girl and this was how I handled it. I had her tell her father that if he didn't start getting here on time, I would give him detention. Tell your father the same thing."

I told him and I was never late again.

Courage --- A Lack of it

Beirne' Beaty

The story I am going to tell took place in 1962. I was a sophomore. It was my first year at Bradley, and I was very intimidated with all the upper classmen. That was the year that Bradley was state champions in football, basketball, softball. They were state champions in everything. These guys especially were really big guys. They were like gods to everybody, so all of the sophomores and freshmen were in awe of them.

For Good Food
. . . Try
**BRADLEY
SNACK SHOP**
Across From the
High School

I was over at the snack shop one day eating lunch (legally) and Mrs. Clemmer started walking across the sidewalk toward the snack shop. I was very much in awe of Mrs. Clemmer because I had heard so much about her.

Suddenly, in the back of the snack shop, it was like popcorn. All these guys who played football and were fearless state champions started running out the back door of the snack shop because Mrs. Clemmer was on her way in. She knew they were on their third lunch break. They were over there and not in class and she was coming over there after them.

It was absolutely hysterical to see them running away from her.

CHAPTER 10

A WOMAN OF FAIRNESS

Fairness: Practicing justice, equity and equality.

Live so that when your children think of fairness and integrity, they think of you.

- H. Jackson Brown, Jr.

Mrs. Inez Clemmer

The Ocoeean 1963

Crime and Punishment

She did her job with grace and fairness.

- Rodney Fitzgerald

Of all the words used to describe Inez Clemmer, interestingly enough, the word "fair" is probably used most often. It is used by those faculty and staff who worked with her. It is used by those students she trained in her work of search, seizure, and recovery. It is even used by those "rascals" who repeatedly experienced the brunt of her fervent conviction that discipline included consequences and accountability.

What a striking commendation! Not necessarily popular, but fair. She was observed to be equal in her treatment of the hundreds of students that passed her way. This meant she was not influenced by social standing, skin color, economic level, or parental power. That in itself would provide some measure of comfort to a quaking student — all ground was level in the detention hall.

It is perhaps this fairness that explains most clearly how it is that Mrs. Clemmer continues to be remembered with such great affection and respect. Being treated fairly is, after all, what matters most to many of us.

Just Compensation

Janet Prueitt Bacon

In 1955, when I was a senior at Bradley Central, and played basketball for Coach Kyle, Mrs. Clemmer played an important part in my life. Coach Kyle was also my Algebra I teacher. My senior year he was sick a lot.

I would be in Mrs. Fitzgerald's 1st Period English and I would hear Mrs. Clemmer call, "Janet Prueitt, please come to the office." She would have me teach Mr. Kyle's Algebra I class. That wasn't all, however. She saw to it that I got paid just like a substitute teacher.

Mrs. Clemmer was my Algebra II teacher. She was about the fairest teacher that I ever knew.

- Maxine Gannaway Hyde

A What? . . . Where?

Alice Rogers

Inez Clemmer had a reputation for fairness, but if you were up to no good, there was at least a "fair" chance you'd be caught and dealt with. As a rather timid student, I was more than glad not to be called into her presence.

However, one morning a tardy arrival at school brought my brother and me into her office. That morning, at our home in rural Bradley County, our path down a rather long driveway to the bus stop was blocked by a Southern Railway freight train.

As soon as we were able to cross the railroad tracks, our mother took us to school with a brief note (too brief). It said simply, "Mrs. Clemmer, Alice and Glenn are late because there was a train across the driveway."

Mrs. Clemmer gave us a funny look and sent us on to class. Later that day, we heard from a friend in her Latin class that Mrs. Clemmer had heard the wildest lie that morning in all her years of teaching --- about a train across the driveway --- and that she'd let us go to class because it was such an incredible story.

A Mistake Corrected

Bobby Owenby

Bobby Owenby even today remembers Mrs. Clemmer's fairness as a disciplinarian. He recalls the day he and a buddy were involved in a classroom activity that took place outside. Believing the activity had been completed, the two returned to school. Shortly after, they were called to the office where Mrs. Clemmer indicated that since they skipped the remainder of the class, they were suspended for three days.

Although he protested the injustice of the suspension, the suspension was ordered. In his upset, Bobby decided not to ride the bus home, but to go straight to his after school job.

When he returned home, his mom told him that Mrs. Clemmer had called, concerned about his failure to board the bus.

She also told his mom about the suspension. He explained to his mom what took place. Later that evening, Mrs. Clemmer called to say that she believed him and he was free to return to school.

Everyone associated or connected with her talked about her fairness, honesty, and above all, her heart.

- Anderson "Jute" Miller

A Fair Response

Linda Lauderdale McNabb

My story is from the early 60's involving desegregation . . . the first year African Americans were allowed at BCHS. That first day of school, George Nerren and I decided to make Terry Scott feel welcome. After school we offered him a ride as he was walking. He accepted the ride and we let him out at the monument.

Before we got home that day, we had threats of burning our house down, running us out of town, etc. My mother was so upset, she thought we would have to move that evening. Of course, someone called Mrs. Clemmer with the news.

She immediately requested that George and I meet at her house with our parents. We decided to take our older sisters (Sylvia Lauderdale and Sally Nerren) since they had such a good reputation with Mrs. Clemmer and knew her well.

George and I were shaking with fear, but Mrs. Clemmer did not punish us in any way. She thought what we did was a nice gesture, perhaps just too soon. We made it through the night without incident, and, after a few days, things calmed back down. Terry Scott won everyone over with his basketball ability and made a lot of friends before the year's end. A few years ago he was honored with a "Terry Scott Day".

This story shows the fairness and firmness that made Mrs. Clemmer stand out among administrators of Tennessee.

George Nerren

We had study hall in the old auditorium. It was like a human warehouse, with 200-300 students seated in uncomfortable chairs. One day I ran to the medical center pharmacy between classes, bought a pint of ice cream, and slipped into my seat in study hall.

I had only eaten a few bites before I was caught by the teacher and sent to Mrs. Clemmer's office. Her first reaction was to ask me if I had an extra spoon for her. Then she laughed with me and said, "You know I'm going to give you detention for this, don't you?"

I said, "Yes maam". She gave me an hour's detention and then told me to stay in her office until I had finished my ice cream. She was an understanding, caring person with a sense of humor, firm yet flexible and fair.

Mistaken Identity

Sarah Lou Goins Coffey

I was at Bradley High School from 1942 to 1946. I never did have Mrs. Clemmer as a teacher, but I worked with her quite a bit when she was a vice principal. When my daughter began attending Bradley, I told her she only needed to worry about Mrs. Clemmer if she was mean; those who misbehaved got caught. I said, "Keep your nose clean and you'll be fine."

Well, she was called to the office. Mrs. Clemmer jumped on her like a rooster on a June bug, telling her that she had laid out of class too many times and all.

My daughter's name was Phyllis Elaine Coffey. Phyllis kept telling her that she had not been out of school. It was Phyllis E. Collins records she was looking at.

Mrs. Clemmer apologized. Phyllis never did get into any more trouble and I told her not to take advantage.

She was strict, but fair; stern, but compassionate.
*   - Maureen Olsson Lovelace*

Justice

Ralph Chase

My chief recollection of Mrs. Clemmer is of her calling me to her office for many different reasons. I thought they would wear the intercom system out with my name. She always listened to my side of the story and was very helpful in my getting through graduation.

Even the worst rascal knew she was fair.

- Eugenia Rodgers

Andrew Bennett

A student was walking down the hall using a variety of profanities. A teacher was nearby and appeared about to correct the student. Mrs. Clemmer touched her on the arm and said, "If you knew how far this young man has come, you might just want to let it go."

After twenty-eight years of teaching, not a year goes by that I don't think of her and her fairness.

- Valerie Hyberger Williams

The Ocoeean 1958

CHAPTER 11

A MYSTERIOUS OMNISCIENCE

The students used to call Mrs. Clemmer "The FBI Agent" because when something happened she would find out who was responsible.

- Rodney Fitzgerald

One recurring theme throughout the gathering of "Clemmer stories" has been the incomprehensible ability of Mrs. Clemmer to "know" the actions, whereabouts, and guilt of BCHS students. The underlying question accompanying many stories was "How did she know that?"

One answer could perhaps be found in the old platitude that "God looks out for fools and children" --- some Bradley students were perhaps a little bit of both. Apparently Mrs. Clemmer was His instrument of choice for "looking out for them". There is also, of course, something to be said for the truth of the adage "be sure your sins will find you out".

Then again, some things are just beyond knowing. Did she have a sixth sense, a "Jiminy Cricket" type ally? What we do know is her "mysterious omniscience" resulted in the capture or exposure of some of Bradley's most notorious (and mischievous) students!

The Invisible Woman?

Brenda Beaty Remine

It was a beautiful spring day and some of us decided to cut afternoon classes and head to the lake . . . so we met in the parking lot. Without thinking, I turned right and was driving in front of the school. Lo and behold, who was standing on the steps, but Inez! So, I hollered, "DUCK!" and everyone lay down. I scrunched down behind the wheel out of sight and made it past her. We laughed and laughed!! Until the next morning when she called me into her office and said, "That is quite a car you have. I didn't know that it could drive itself until I saw it go by yesterday." I could have fallen over because we thought we had made a clean getaway . . . and, of course, she knew who else was in the car . . . she called them into her office as well and handed out detention. She wasn't interested in the "forged excuses".

I do not remember EVER getting away with anything. She had eyes in the back of her head and knew everything about everybody . . . an amazing lady, but always fair.

I was visiting Suzanne Allen one day (she lives across from Mrs. Clemmer's house). Inez was out in the yard, and I had not seen her in years. She greeted me warmly and I said how much I had enjoyed high school. She said, "It didn't appear that way, you were always trying to escape!!!" We had a big laugh.

Just about everyone was caught by Mrs. Clemmer at one point or another because she would catch you no matter how sly you were.
- Janice Slaughter Gregg

Facing the "Music"

Joe Hamilton

My dad, J. Paul Hamilton attended Bradley High School in 1964. Because he was known as a class clown, he became well acquainted with Inez Clemmer.

Mrs. Clemmer was supervising study hall one day when a twaanng . . . rang out, sounding something like the string of a guitar being plucked. J.Paul had asked one of the female students for a hair pin that he straightened out, inserted between the edge of his seat and its frame, and plucked with his thumb making the loud twaanng . . . causing the whole study hall to burst out laughing.

As J. Paul told it later, "Mrs. Clemmer had her back to the class so I really thought I could get away with something this time. I put on my best innocent act and like everyone else just laughed and looked around the room, like I was trying to see whoever had created the disturbance.

It was amazing. The lady turned around, looked straight in my direction, and walked to my seat. She looked at me with those black eyes, arms folded behind her, and said, 'J.Paul, I want whatever contraption you have put together to make that noise placed on my desk as you leave study hall. I will discuss your punishment with Coach Sullivan. I'm sure there is something extra he can have you do on the football practice field which will serve as a reminder not to disrupt study hall again.'

From then on, Mrs. Clemmer was always known to me and others as the lady with eyes in the back of her head. I never did try to put anything over on her again."

You hear stories "my mother has eyes in the back of her head and she knows everything I do". Well, to me that was the way Mrs. Clemmer was. She knew who did what and there was no sense trying to lie out of it.

- Dianne Bitty May Brogden

The Eyes are Watching

Glendon Morgan Belk

It was like she had eyes everywhere. This story is about some of my best friends and me. We checked out of school early. Mrs. Clemmer did the attendance. Her husband worked at Dixie Foundry and my best friend's mother worked at Dixie Foundry. And Mrs. Clemmer's husband took my best friend's mother to work, so Mrs. Clemmer knew her real well.

One day we checked out of school to study. We were not skipping class, we were studying. The next day Mrs. Clemmer checked the attendance sheet and she saw where we had checked out and she called us all into her office.

She said, "Girls, I want you to be made aware that I knew you had checked out. I know you weren't playing hooky, but I want you to know that I know when you come and go."

You couldn't get away with anything that she was not aware of!

A Cold Shoulder

Deborah Humberd Kimsey

As a Clemmer office aide, working in Mrs. Clemmer's office never gave us any leeway because we were held to an even higher standard. I did make the major mistake of running over to the Zesto for ice cream cones once, with the other aide, supposedly, acting as the lookout. We had waited until Mrs. Clemmer was making a parking lot surveillance run.

We thought we had plenty of time to accomplish this minute task. I was standing there waiting at the window while the guy fixed the cones when he suddenly froze with the ice cream scoop mid-air. With a chill down my spine, I finally said, "She's standing right behind me, isn't she?" He slowly nodded his head.

He was nice enough to give me my money back before we both (Mrs. Clemmer and I) walked across the street with her arm draped across my shoulder. That "shoulder drape" was her way of taking opportunity to talk to us while avoiding our escape. That arm was stronger than any wrestler's arm. To this day, I still think there were actually ten of her, as there was **no** way she could always be in that many different places. It was amazing!

Oh Be Careful, Little Feet

Roy Morris

Mrs. Clemmer was everywhere. Once I saw Mrs. Clemmer at the end of the hall, so I *ran* downstairs to get to class. When I got to the bottom, Mrs. Clemmer was there waiting for me. She made me *walk* back up the stairs and *walk* back down them again.

> *She had eyes that would go through you. They got the job done.*
>
> *- Eddie Nicholson*

CHAPTER 12

MRS. INEZ CLEMMER...

STORIES WORTH TELLING

Lessons, Laughter, and Tough Love: The Inez Clemmer Legacy was written as a support resource for the character traits curriculum endorsed by the Bradley County School System. In the process of gathering "Clemmer stories", it was discovered that some really good stories just weren't going to fit in one of the nine chapters designating a character trait.

However, in line with *Lessons, Laughter, and Tough Love*, these stories were still very much worth including in a book about Inez Clemmer. For another component of this book is that, in telling Clemmer stories, we are also telling the story of a community and of the people that have populated this community for several decades.

Shocked?

Mike Harris

I was in Mrs. Buckner's class. I sat on the back row near the wall. There was a 220 volt outlet on the wall near my desk.
I opened up a paper clip, wrapped a piece of paper around it and shorted out the outlet. Sparks flew all over the room. Everybody was scared to death. I was definitely in trouble, but glad to be alive. I got to meet Mrs. Clemmer. I think this was the first time I ever had detention.

Brains, Not Brawn

Conrad Day

During my time at Bradley, I did not have Mrs. Clemmer for a teacher --- but I knew her as most everyone did. During the time I was manager of the B&B Supermarket, I occasionally called on her for a "good bag boy", someone who needed a job and was trustworthy. This particular occasion she sent me a boy she said was reliable, honest, and needed a job. This boy *was* a good one, but after working only a couple of days with me, he resigned. His statement and reason for quitting was this: "This job of bagging groceries is just not for me. I'll find something that suits me better." Well, the boy *did* find something else. He went on into life and later became wealthy using his head instead of his back! The boy was Franklin Haney.

Mercy

Max Finkle

It was May, 1963 and only two days of school left. A group of us got in some trouble with a teacher who was the recipient of a practical joke intended for a student. The teacher gave us a week of detention that would have prevented us from graduating. We were terrified when Mrs. Clemmer called us into the office. We walked in there and she couldn't keep a straight face. I have never seen her laugh like that. She shortened our detention which allowed us to graduate.

No Mercy

Denny Williams

The only experience I had with Mrs. Clemmer was in the school year '69-70. I had a flat tire on the way to school and I knew how Mrs. Clemmer was. She was strict. I had to stop at the gas station to have it fixed. I asked the guy at the service station if he could give me a receipt or something indicating that I had a flat tire 'cause I knew what I would face when I got to school. So he made out a receipt saying I had a flat tire. Luckily, my brother got into his homeroom, but my homeroom was right next to Mrs. Clemmer's office.

When I tried to go into my homeroom late, I heard "Dennis". The only other time I heard that name was when my mother called me that and I knew I was in trouble. I knew right then I was going to have a hard time.

I went in and said "Mrs. Clemmer, I had a flat tire and here is an excuse from the service station." But there was no excuse for tardiness as far as Mrs. Clemmer was concerned.

I thought I would never forget the feeling of my heart dropping when she started writing on that yellow piece of paper because yellow was unexcused – pink was excused. And Mrs. Clemmer gave me 30 minutes detention for having that flat tire. That was probably the only time I had detention the whole time I was there.

No Fun for this Blonde

Gail Billig Walker

I went to Bradley High from 1968 to 1971. During my sophomore year I had a blonde wig. I, however, am a brunette. I wore the blonde wig to school one day and my homeroom teacher didn't recognize me so she marked me absent. Well, I had gotten all the way to fifth period when Mr. Montgomery, my biology teacher, said, "Gail, you aren't supposed to be here today. You are on the absentee list."

I said, "No, I have been here all day. It was this stupid blonde wig. My homeroom teacher didn't know who I was."

So I had to go to Mrs. Clemmer's office and tell her that I had been counted absent all day because my homeroom teacher didn't recognize me

She thought it was funny, but I was so humiliated by that blonde wig that I never wore it again.

Fireworks!

Don Akins

I was in homeroom with Mickey Atchley. We were there early one morning. Mickey had some "booby traps". These are little firecracker that have a string coming out both ends. If a string is tied to something that pulls the strings out, it sets off the firecracker. Mickey thought he would booby trap the doors leading to the auditorium where the freshmen girls had homeroom. I went with him to see if he would really do it.

When he really started tying them to the handles, I decided it was time for Don to get out of there. As he was tying the last string, a teacher appeared on the inside of the door. She took Mickey and his booby traps to Mrs. Clemmer.

Later, Mickey showed up in homeroom looking like a ghost. Toward the end of homeroom, he was called back to the office. Mrs. Clemmer had pulled one of the strings while holding the firecracker in the other hand. It went off!!

Poor Mickey must have been called to her office a half dozen times that day. I am soooo glad I decided to get out of there!

Thwarted!

Andrew Bennett

My brother Swanson threw a snowball at the school and Mrs. Clemmer caught him. She told him he was going to have to serve detention that afternoon.

He replied, "That's good, I won't have to milk."

Mrs. Clemmer responded, "Swanson, you go right on home now."

Miffed!

Jimmie Ruth Gregg Leis

In my sophomore year, my cousin Roy Sherlin skipped school and he asked me to write him a note. So, being a loving cousin, I wrote him a note, saying he was sick and was home in bed. I signed it Mrs. Sherlin.

The next day Mrs. Clemmer called me into her office and she said, "Have a seat, Mrs. Sherlin. I have something to discuss with you." Needless to say, I almost fainted.

I never, ever wrote another note for anybody. I could not believe my cousin ratted on me! Do you believe it? Do a favor and he rats on me!

Illegal Concessions

Mike Harris

I worked in the projector room at school during fifth period. One day two of us decided to go to the popcorn stand during that time. We took two empty film projector cases and filled one with popcorn and one with cokes.

As we were going back to the building, Mrs. Austin asked us where we had been. We said we were just taking these film strip projectors back to the projector room. He wanted to see in the cases.

I got to see Mrs. Clemmer again. I can't remember if I got detention for this escapade, but it was our last popcorn run.

Prophecies

Gladys Tye

I'll never forget and have had a lot of laughs when I remember Mrs. Clemmer said, "Now, Randy, I know you made an "A" in Latin I last year at Arnold, but you'll have to take it over this year. You just don't know it."

Bob Ervin

Shortly before his high school graduation in 1953, Mrs. Clemmer asked Bob Ervin a pointed question. "Tell me the truth, did you *ever* take a schoolbook home?"

Bob answered the question honestly. "No, I didn't."

Mrs. Clemmer responded confidently, "You will regret it."

Fifty three years later, Mr. Ervin acknowledges the accuracy of her words. He says, "She was right. I have certainly regretted it."

- as told to Lettie Burress

Quiet Down There!

Bill McMahan

I had Mrs. Clemmer for Algebra I and II in the early fifties. Her classroom was over the boys' locker room. Sometimes the boys would become loud, singing songs, and making lots of noise. Mrs. Clemmer would hit on the floor to quiet them.

Sensible Solutions

Bettie Bledsoe Goldhagen

The only dealing I ever had with Mrs. Clemmer was once when I became ill. She sent me home in a taxi, along with a huge cafeteria-size vegetable tin can in case I upchucked on the way. She told me to be sure and return the can to her the next morning (the last thing a teenage girl wanted to be carrying through the halls).

Five Fortunate Years

Jack Easterly

I was one of the fortunate few to have five years at BCHS with Mrs. Clemmer. I was down to the finals, had my cap and gown, invitations sent out, and then failed senior English with a 73 average. A friend with a 77 thought I could have two of his extra points to pass, but by Mrs. Fitzgerald laughed at that. I had a good time those five years and would do it again.

I was always in a lot of trouble. It was nothing mean or that caused harm, but was just clean fun. I'd hang out at Bob's Billiards or I'd climb out the window after roll was taken in P.E. and go to the snack shop for three lunch periods. The snack shop was also a good place to head sixth period, when we could eat all the leftover sandwiches from lunch.

I deserved everything that I got, but I did get away with one thing. On the first day of the school year, we would write our names down for class roll. Some of us liked to put down false names like George Washington. Once, I signed Herman Jones in three or four classes. Someone would answer "Here" for a few days, and then the name would finally appear on the absentee list. Mrs. Clemmer came to study hall looking for "Herman Jones", because he couldn't be found and no one knew of him. Heads were turned toward me, but I didn't get caught.

Another incident took place in the evening. I had a truck and another buddy had a truck. We would load up with ten or fifteen kids and drive back and forth between Lon's Snack Shop on North Ocoee and Sugar 'N' Spice on South Lee to see who was there and what was going on. We started throwing eggs, mostly at each other. The other truck was stopped and fifteen kids were taken to jail. I took my truckload down to the jail. The jail windows were open because there was no air-conditioning. We were climbing in and out of the jail windows until they sent us all home.

The next day, Mrs. Clemmer was on the intercom asking everyone who was involved in the truck deal to report to her office and that she had their names. There were so many that we were in the hall outside her office. Some were hoodlums, but some were her best and favorite students. She threw up her hands, said, "Don't do this again!", and let us go.

Another incident took place on one of my many visits to Mrs. Clemmer's office. A boy came in with his inseam ripped out. He was insisting on going home. Instead, Mrs. Clemmer got out a needle and thread to sew up his pants, and back to class he went.

Beyond BCHS

Sylvia Lauderdale Coates

Over the years, Mrs. Clemmer became part of our family. Our sons, Eddie and Tanner, visited her with us from the time they were three or four years old. It was routine for them, even during their college years. One day in particular, defined what a great mind she had and what a magnificent lady she was. As she was talking to them, she said, "Boys, you know I am always happy when your mother stops by to see me, but I want to know something. How old are you now?" When they answered fourteen and fifteen, she continued, "Well, I know a 14 or 15 year old teenager would rather be anywhere in the world than visiting a 90 year old woman. I thank and appreciate you for coming to see me." She still had Eddie's autographed tennis poster from Vanderbilt near her rocking chair at her death.

Inez at home December 1993

Sarah Parks, Neighbor

When I was in school, I called her Mrs. Clemmer and could not even think of calling her by her first name as an adult. One day she said, "You call me Mrs. Clemmer. Why not Inez?"

We laughed about such things as Inez, at 90, getting a phone call from a dating service! She called me saying that she was ahead of me.

Anna Thomas, Sarah Parks and Inez Clemmer

Anna Lee Thomas, Neighbor

We knew that Mrs. Clemmer had many of her old students to visit. Inez invited one man to come in and, after a long visit, he told her that she was very cordial and he had enjoyed talking to her, but he was there to sell her an Electrolux.

To her surprise, he wasn't a student after all.

Ruthanna Stratton Almond

My daughter Ann and I visited Mrs. Clemmer in her home about two weeks before her death. We found her very alert and happy. Our conversation was mostly about her years of teaching at Polk County School and Bradley High. She had a stack of yearbooks near her chair to which she referred for years and dates.

Walter Presswood

When I visited Mrs. Clemmer, she always gave me two or three books to take with me. One of the last batches of books that she gave me had been published that year. One of them was funny bedtime stories. I don't remember what the main purpose of that book was, but it was a funny book. She had a great sense of humor.

Don Geren

Just before Mrs. Clemmer died, I ran into her in the lobby of the doctor's office, walked over and said, "I know you won't remember me, but I need to say something to you." As sharp as ever, she said, "Sit down here Don Geren, and let's talk." I was amazed she could still remember me! I was able to tell her in person I appreciated her and felt that God had directed me back then and now.

Suzanne Cunnyngham Allen

Many Bradley graduates probably thought when Mrs. Clemmer retired, her influence was over. Living across the street, I know better. I often saw her in the yard with neighborhood children and know that those lucky children had the good fortune of being exposed to her experience, guidance, and knowledge.

Being retired was too strong a word. She never retired or slowed down.

Margaret Cate /Nina Jensen

During the last twenty years of her life, Mrs. Clemmer frequently played duplicate bridge with our Monday afternoon group. She was sharp as a tack and loved to bid 3NT which she always made while others foundered in a suit.

To this day, whenever anyone bids no trump someone will say, "Alright, Inez." She was such a delightful lady who never got upset and if one of us did, she would always say, "Now", and call us by name.

We do miss her gentle spirit and keen mind.

Gail Kerr Kearns

I may have been the last of her former students to come back and see her before she passed away. I was in Cleveland on May 13, 2000 for the first time in more than twenty years. I called Mrs. Clemmer on the phone. "Do you remember me?" I asked.

"Of course I remember you! Come right on over!" And so I did. Almost forty years had gone by since my graduation from Bradley. I brought my husband and my youngest daughter. We all had a delightful conversation and passed a fine afternoon with this wonderful 95-year-old lady, who was as sharp and interesting as I had known her to be so many long years ago. We visited Mrs. Clemmer on Saturday. On Monday, suddenly, she was gone.

Rest in peace, Mrs.Clemmer. Neither you nor your teaching will ever be forgotten. As your students cross this land, they take more than a bit of you with them wherever they go and to whatever they do. And many of them, as you knew, have also chosen to be teachers!

The Ocoeean, 1969

Inez Clemmer Library Committee

James Floyd- Librarian

Ron Spangler - Principal

Mr. & Mrs. Gary Smith

Alan Smith

Leslie Christian

Lettie Burress

Nancy Eskew

Tracy Hamilton

Sandy Wallis

About the Project

Every major successful project is first envisioned, and then accomplished. This book about Inez Clemmer had several visionaries who worked patiently and productively toward the final goal of the publication of this material.

It has been a project under construction for several years, beginning in January, 2002. But *Lessons, Laughter, and Tough Love: The Inez Clemmer Legacy* is only one part of a process whose outcome has been the funding, designing, decorating, and updating of one of the most creative, enjoyable, and enticing middle school libraries in the area. In May, 2001, the Bradley County Board of Education voted to rename the Ocoee Middle School Library in honor of Inez Clemmer. The support of the Board, OMS PTO, community, and family has allowed the Inez Clemmer Library to be transformed into a pleasing and inviting environment.

A volunteer group of committed visionaries has overseen the beginning and ending of this book project, with proceeds going to benefit the library. This memory project team consists of James Floyd, the librarian at Ocoee Middle School, Traci Hamilton, former PTO president and Sandy Wallis, who served on the Bradley County Board of Education. Each one, interestingly enough, has been uniquely suited to play an indispensable role in the book-making process.

These three have given countless hours of their time to the process of meeting, working, and organizing the efforts that resulted in the "birth" of this book. Without their contributions, it wouldn't have been possible. Only those closely involved can comprehend the "responsibility", "self-discipline" and "perseverance" they have demonstrated. It so clearly reflected their "caring" for the students of Ocoee Middle School and the "respect" they have for the value of reading and learning which was an integral part of the Inez Clemmer legacy.

A huge debt of gratitude is owed to this team, the driving force behind this book. In providing *Lessons, Laughter, and Tough Love: The Inez Clemmer Legacy*, they dreamed big and have given this community a resource to treasure.

Inez Clemmer
Student Memory Project Participants
2003

Katie Melton, Makayla Walker, Jennifer Jenkins, Zach Spurlin,
Audra Wallis, Alex Clark, Brook Hines, Harry McMahan

2006

Sarah Wright, Katie Smith, Shelby Pankey, Alex Lawson,
Noah Stallings, Kyle Dockery, Miles Christian, Drew Zaleta,
Heather Morrow, Andrew Lawson, Brody Hambright, Caleb Taylor

Memory Contributors

Don Akins, 1968

Peggy Turner Allen, 1961

Suzanne Cunnyngham Allen, 1960

Ruth Stratton Almond, 1934, PCHS

Bill Arnold, M.D., 1963

Janet Prueitt Bacon, 1955

Beirne` Beaty, 1966

Glendon Morgan Belk, 1960

Andrew F. Bennett, Jr., 1956

Don Bivens, 1957

Dianne Biddy May Brogden, 1962-1963

Stony Brooks, 1963

Jack Brown, 1950

Robert "Bob" Burris, 1962

Joyce Orr Bush, 1952

Eddie Cartwright, 1954

Milteen Hornsby Cartwright, 1955

Margaret Cate, Bridge player

Ralph Chase, 1955

Leslie Smith Christian, Great-niece

John Climer, Jr., Early 1960's

Sylvia Lauderdale Coates, 1962

Sarah Lou Goins Coffey, 1946

Paul Conn, 1963

Norma Davis Coppinger, 1959

Jeannie Callaway-Crocco, 1953

Blair Cunnyngham, Businessman

Cordie Evans Davis, 1958

Connie Day, 1960

Conrad Day, Businessman, Cartoonist

Josephine Seaton Day, 1941

Jack Easterly 1958,1959
La Verne Bennett Easterly, 1959

Bob Ervin, 1953

Brenda Evans, 1963

Vernon "Clem" Fannin, 1958

Carolyn Brewer Ferguson, 1969

Max Finkle, 1963

Rodney Fitzgerald, 1964

Jerry Frazier, 1966, Superintendent Bradley County Schools

Don M. Geren, 1957

Steve Gibson, 1962

Caroline Lacy Goins, 1968

Rebecca Hysinger Goins, 1971

Betty Bledsoe Goldenhagen, 1958

Marsha King Goodwin, BCHS 1965

Johnny Gregg
Janice Slaughter Gregg, 1958

Oney Dodd Hambright, 1949

Joe Hamilton, 1970

J. Paul Hamilton, 1949

Mike Harris, 1968

Nora Varnell Hilburn, 1949

Buddy Houlk, BCHS mid-1950's

Maxine Gannaway Buckner Hyde,
1950

Nina Jensen, Bridge player

Peggy Hurst Johnson, 1952

Tom Johnson, 1969

Vesta Guthrie Jones, 1968

Gail Kerr Kearns, 1962

Deborah Humberd Kimsey, 1969

Glenda Bryant Kyker, 1959

Herbert Lackey, 1957

Tommy Lee, 1955

Jimmie Ruth Greg Leis, 1954

Maureen Olsson Lovelace, 1958

Bill McClure, 1958

Linda Mital McConnell, 1964

Evelyn McCurry, BCHS

Mildred Miller McGuire, 1958

Bill McMahan, BCHS early 1950's

Brenda Simmons McLain, 1960

Linda Lauderdale McNabb, 1966

Alfred Melton, 1959

Betty Melton Gamble, BCHS

Anderson "Jute" Miller, 1960

Linda Elkins Moore, 1965

Kathy Murray Morelock, 1970

Roy Morris, BCHS 1963-1964

Gerdline Mull, BCHS

George Nerren, 1966

Eddie Nicholson, 1948

Gaytha Bradley Ogle, 1964

Bernie Orr, 1955

Bobby Owenby, 1959

Sarah Parks, Neighbor

Janey Parton, 1969

Dick Pelley, 1960

Johnny Pickett
Rachel Nunley Pickett, 1962

Ann Almond Pope, 1958

Walter Presswood,
Bradley County Board of Education

Sheridan Randolph, 1964

Steve Ratterman,
Friend of BCHS students

Mary Manges Reeves, 1966

Brenda Beaty Remine, 1958

Harold Reno, BCHS faculty

Eugenia Rodgers, BCHS faculty

Chris Rodie, 1966

Alice Rogers, 1970

(James) Ronald Rogers, 1955

Jeanne Harshbarger Sawyer, 1953

Bill Schultz, BCHS Principal

Jeanette Manly Schlaeger, 1962

Marty Fulbright Semmes, 1958

Joy Self Shook, 1965

Berta McReynolds Silcox, 1961

Steve Sloan, 1962

Alan Smith, Great-nephew

Don Smith, Nephew/ 1953

Gary Smith, Nephew/ 1955

Marguerite Miles Smith, 1958

Patsy Coker Smith, 1965

Edward Sneed, Parent, 1967

Dennis Spurlin, Neighbor

Janice Crye Suits, 1965

G.P. (Jeep) Tulloss, 1949

Anna Lee Thomas. Neighbor

Gladys Tye, Parent, 1961

Markolita Still Vaden, 1960

Gail Billig Walker, 1971

Denny Williams, 1972

Valerie Hyberger Williams, 1969

Doris Ann Webb Wright, 1957

Phyllis Nichols Wright, 1963

Credits

Cleveland Daily Banner:

"A gifted, respected teacher – stern, fair, and loved" –
Lifestyles (Nancy Carney) February 24, 1985

"How did she always know" – (Nancy Carney)

"A grand lady is being honored" –
Editorial (Beecher Hunter) March 6, 1985

"To students she was both disciplinarian and friend" –
Personality Profile (Nancy Carney) March 10, 1985

Appreciation Book: Presented to Inez Clemmer on
March 8, 1985 at the Inez Clemmer
Scholarship Dinner

The Ocoeean: 1944, 1945, 1946, 1952, 1954, 1956, 1957, 1958,
1959, 1962, 1963, 1964, 1966, 1967, 1968, 1969

Photos: Inez and Lee Clemmer family
Gary and Marguerite Smith family
Sara Parks and Anna Lee Parks Thomas
Valerie Hyberger Williams
Bron Herron McEachern Photographers
(Mural photo)

Cartoons: Conrad Day

Character trait definitions: "Character is Cool"
Character Education Program
Bradley County Schools

Inez Clemmer Scholarship Dinner (Video-recording)
March 8, 1985